T0370438

The **SMILEY LEADERSHIP** and **MENTORING EXPERIENCE**

For Faith Based Entrepreneurs and Small Business Leaders

PAUL A. SMILEY

authorHOUSE

AuthorHouse™
1663 Liberty Drive
Bloomington, IN 47403
www.authorhouse.com
Phone: 833-262-8899

Published by AuthorHouse 05/17/2024

ISBN: 979-8-8230-2649-9 (sc)
ISBN: 979-8-8230-2650-5 (hc)
ISBN: 979-8-8230-2648-2 (e)

Library of Congress Control Number: 2024909892

Print information available on the last page.

This book is printed on acid-free paper.

CONTENTS

DEDICATION

This book is dedicated to the past, present, and future Smiley-Butler-Moore Family, and to all the amazing people I have encountered on this life journey. Words cannot express how much I value and appreciate each one of you for being a part of my life.

Keep the faith,
Paul

FOREWORD BY RYAN NUNEZ, PHD

Leaders who use their position of authority for their own benefit cause some of the greatest problems in the world today. These corrupt leaders use and manipulate the people they lead to meet their own personal goals and agenda. While we typically think of corrupt leadership within the realm of government officials or political operatives, we are more likely to encounter unethical leadership in the workplace. You will see a supervisor or manager using others to move up the ranks and advance their career. Oftentimes, a CEO will squeeze the last bit of profit out of their company at the expense of their employees' wellbeing.

We see the negative effects of poor leadership in so many facets of our lives. Families can also be susceptible to the impacts of corrupt leadership. When a parent or elder leads through manipulation, guilt, or shame, it can leave a pathway of pain and trauma that carries over from childhood into adulthood. So how can we remedy poor leadership? The antidote to corrupt leadership is servant leadership. A servant leader puts the needs of the people they are entrusted to lead above their own. They lead for the benefit of others, not themselves.

For the past 23 years, I have had the privilege of watching Paul Smiley lead in many different capacities. When Paul and I first met, I was a young pastor on staff at Palm Valley Church and he was a Squadron Commander at Luke Air Force Base. His first Sunday attending Palm Valley Church was a shining example of his servant leadership. After service that day, he immediately walked up, introduced himself and asked where he could help. Little did he know that he was an answer to one very specific prayer of our church. We shared our hope and desire to be a multicultural and multigenerational church. Paul understood the importance of people feeling welcomed by someone they could identify with, ethnically and culturally, so he volunteered to join our greeting team. Yes, he was a greeter! Here was a high-capacity leader, a Lieutenant Colonel in the United Stated Air Force, standing outside the church every Sunday greeting every person who came. This is a different kind of leader. I learned so much by watching him lead in the church. Although he was a greeter for many years, he also served as a legal trustee and provided leadership and guidance on many churchwide initiatives and campaigns.

Through the years as I got to know Paul better, I took note of the way he talked about his airmen and his genuine care for their long-term success was evident. I remember when he started Sonoran Technology, he shared the book, *God is My CEO*, with me. It didn't seem like the most opportune time to start any type of company in the midst of the great recession, but his desire to run a business in a different way and lead as a servant was inspiring.

In this latest phase of his leadership career at Sonoran Technology, I have witnessed his servant leadership go into overdrive. I have had the privilege of speaking at several of his annual meetings and met many of his employees. The love they have for Paul is evidence of the type of leader he is. He has helped some of them launch out on their own, not because it was good for his business, but because it was good for them. Countless other business owners have benefited from Paul's mentoring over the years. It is clear he lives out the principles in this book.

In *The Smiley Leadership and Mentoring Experience*, Paul has distilled his years of leadership experience into seven principles that every leader needs to know. My hope and prayer is that as you read them, you will be inspired to put the principles into practice. Whether you lead one or thousands, the people you lead will benefit from it, and by the way, you will too!

Right Place, Right Time

First, I want to thank you for reading this book. I have wanted to write this book, ***The Smiley Leadership and Mentoring Experience***, and tell my small business ownership story for a long time. However, I just wasn't ready. Now I'm ready, and hopefully this book finds you at exactly the right time in your entrepreneurial journey.

Experience and my faith have taught me this: *"God has a plan and that everything happens right on time."* Maybe this book, for example, found its way to you just when you needed it. Maybe you gravitated to it yourself, or somebody that cares about you gave it to you–yet regardless of how you came across it, we found each other in the right place, at the right time.

If you're going through a rough time, something I call a valley, in life, how you manage those valleys is what counts. If you are a "believer," you already know we will be tested, but He will also provide the strength we need to deal with it. There will be times in life where it feels like things are not happening on schedule. Things such as love, success, family, or health for example.

I believe this also means there is no wrong places or wrong times. There have been several moments in my life, and in my family's life, where something happened off schedule. As I patiently waited and gave God time to play His plan out, those moments were exactly what I needed.

As you read, I encourage you to think about moments in your life where things seemed to happen at the "wrong time," and reflect on how those moments were probably all part of His greater plan.

> "There is an appointed time for everything. And there is a time for every event under heaven—"[1]
> (Ecclesiastes 3:16)

CHICAGO, ILLINOIS, 1971-

As a kid, I loved playing baseball.

It was the summer of 1971 on Chicago's west side, I was 12-years old. I was a better than average ball player, and I most enjoyed pitching and playing first base. Our team, the Troy Street Expos, was made up of the boys from my neighborhood – an eclectic group of friends that reflected the West Garfield area we grew up in. We had all sorts of ethnicities and heritages on our block, Jewish families, Italian families, Puerto Rican families, Black families, a unique and wonderful tapestry of diversity. No matter our backgrounds or differences, my friends and I all loved to play baseball.

One summer day in July 1971, my dad bought me a brand-new baseball glove. It was the latest and greatest new glove made in blue and red. We were playing a little league team from what was called the "bad south side" of Chicago. They traveled to the Westside, which I am sure they considered the bad side of town too. One thing was for sure, they brought with them a few unsavory characters.

I was pitching that day, and we won the game. After our

victory, I threw my glove up in the air and ran to the dugout with my friends. We ate potato chips, cookies, and drank pop; it's what some folks on the west coast call soda. All of the sudden, someone from the south-sider area started shooting at random in the park.

My friends and I panicked, and I ran out to the pitcher's mound to grab the glove my dad had just bought me. When I got back to the dugout one of my friends screamed "Paul! You are bleeding!"

I looked down and thought, "I'm going to die." As it turns out, a random .22 caliber bullet had ricocheted off of the batter's cage fence and hit me in my left lower arm near the wrist.

At the time I lived about two blocks from Kells Park which is located on the corner of Kedzie and Chicago Avenue. Between the park and my house was the neighborhood fire station. You would think I ran to the fire station, right? Nope.

I was so freaked out that I just kept running, and running, and running desperately to find that safe place called home.

I ran past the local fire station, and past people trying to help me. My dad was out watering the grass and I ran up to him and I cried out "Dad! I got shot!"

"WHAT?!" he yelled back.

Now just like any parent would be, he was freaking out too. After fumbling to get his car keys, my dad drove me to the local hospital which was about four blocks from our house. Fortunately, the bullet didn't hit any bones or cause any major damage that would prevent me from using my left arm. I spent a few days in the hospital recovering from this horrific and life-changing nightmare with lots of candy from my teammates and friends in the neighborhood.

Before the shooting started after our team's victory, our coach Mr. Malone briefly celebrated with us, and he walked home—Mr. Malone was not at the park when the shooting happened. You can't imagine how out of control those rumors were when they finally made their way back to him.

"Paul got shot seven times in the back of the head!" Poor Mr. Malone almost had a heart attack.

Truth be told, an inch to the left or the right and I could have been one of those hundreds or so shooting fatalities that happen too often in cities, large and small across our country. That miraculous stroke of luck affirmed that yes, God had a plan for me.

I could have easily written it off that I was in the wrong place at the wrong time. Not true. I was in the right place at the right time! I was a 12-year-old kid doing what 12-year-old kids in my neighborhood loved to do, play baseball with their friends on a beautiful summer day! This near tragedy did not stop me from playing sports with my friends, in fact, I loved baseball that much more. I continued to play sports all through high school, and what I learned playing sports helped mold me into the person I am today. Virtues such as family, teamwork, resilience, and humility (i.e. losing is not fatal), are things I treasure today. Who knows, if had I let the shooting stop me from playing team sports, would I still have those virtues today?

It is important to realize that whenever we face adversity to remind ourselves God has a plan. I'm confident we are meant to be here on this Earth for some purpose. Maybe you're not sure what it is, or like musical artist Danny Gokey sings in one of my favorite songs, *Haven't Seen It Yet*:

"It's like the brightest sunrise

Waiting on the other side of the darkest night
Don't ever lose hope, hold on and believe
Maybe you just haven't seen it, just haven't seen it yet
You're closer than you think you are
Only moments from the break of dawn
All His promises are just up ahead ..."[2]

Let me share with you another example of a time when I used to think, "wow, that happened at the wrong time and the wrong place," before I made sense of it and realized that God had a greater plan for me.

CHICAGO, 1977-

When I was in high school, we had a high school senior class of about three hundred students. I was ranked around number thirty-three academically and I was going to go to college, hopefully play in the jazz band, and I was scheduled to take the ACT test the spring of 1977. At this moment in time, the Air Force was not really something I had considered, even though my dad, his five brothers, and several uncles on my mom's side of the family had served honorably in WW II and the Korean War.

I labored over preparing for the ACT. At that time there were no on-line study guides or tutorials, just telephone book sized study guides you purchased at a bookstore in the mall. Nonetheless, I was determined to be the second in my family to go to college and take advantage of all the sacrifices and hard work my parents and grandparents had put into giving me the opportunity to succeed. Truth be told, I was not particularly excited about taking the ACT, because my fellow classmates and

I had heard it was a tough test. However, I was well aware how important it was and the impact it would have on getting into college.

It is early Saturday morning, showtime, test time, and my friends and I are pumped and ready! Then, in the middle of the math portion of the test, I got sick. I left the testing facility to go to the restroom; you can probably figure out why. When I returned, I was told by one of the teachers in charge of the test facility, "I'm sorry young man, once you leave the testing facility you are not permitted to return." Instantly, panic set in. How could this happen? Why did I get sick now? This is all happening at the wrong place and at the wrong time!

The following week, an Air Force recruiter came to our high school to participate in a career day. I noticed him and several military recruiters canvassing the hallways but, I was really impressed with the Air Force recruiter. He had a sharp but non-intimidating professional demeanor along with a look of confidence and strength. He looked like he could be on a military recruiting poster.

I introduced myself to him and shortly after, I began to tell him about the ACT situation. He said, "Listen, I understand your situation, but this is not the right place to talk about your career ambitions. When you can, find some time when you and your dad can come to my office, and we can talk about your future."

A few weeks later, my dad and I went downtown to the Chicago recruiting station to meet with the Air Force recruiter. I can clearly remember how straightforward the recruiter was. He said, "Paul, you can go into the Air Force and stay four years, or eight years, or make a career out of it." He paused, "or you can come out as an alcoholic." At first his words shocked me. Then

I remembered there was a young man on our block who went into the Army six or seven years earlier, and just like the recruiter said, he left the military with a major drinking problem. The Air Force recruiter further explained that the Air Force would offer me boundless opportunities. "We are going to open the door, and you are going to walk through the door. Whatever happens after that is up to you–you must do the work."

I thought about it for what seemed like an eternity.

I knew going into the Air Force had some advantages, because my dad, who was my hero, was an Army Korean War combat veteran, and I had uncles who all served either in the Army, the Navy, and the Air Force. On July 22, 1977, I decided to take what would be my first leap of faith and walk through the Air Force door and serve something larger than myself; my country. Immediately after finishing basic training and technical school, I enrolled in local colleges on base and began taking as many night courses as my work schedule would allow. I took every College Level Examination Program (CLEP) test possible. The point of this story? My high school classmates graduated from college in the summer of 1981. I graduated college in August of 1982 – just one year after them, even after serving in the Air Force full time. Because I got sick and had to leave the testing facility on that Saturday morning in the spring of 1977, that particular Air Force recruiter ended up in my path. Turns out, I got sick at the right place at the right time. God had a plan. I answered the call He sent me and began my life journey as an adult.

At 18 years old it became clear that God had a uniquely designed plan for my life. I began to reflect on the people in my life that had those "wrong place, wrong time," moments and realized how in fact they were the right place and right time moments for them, and eventually, for me too.

Those moments start with my heritage.

My grandfather and grandmother owned about forty acres of land in central Mississippi. The Hebert and Gazetta Smiley family only worked on their land. Eventually, the land was passed down to my dad and his seven siblings. Today, the land is still owned by the Smiley-Butler-Moore Family.

During the Great Depression (August 1929 to 1939), our grandmother would tell us about life in the South during those horrific years. My grandfather Herbert Smiley, Sr., was a farmer, a tailor for men's clothes, and rumor has it, he did a little "moonshining" on the side—today we would call that the "gig economy." A somewhat short man, my grandfather had a jolly but intimidating personality. He always had a car and, although he could not drive, his sons (including my dad) and his daughter-in law were his chauffeurs.

My grandfather's character and standing in the community were important examples to set for my dad and uncles because when my grandfather went to town, he was acknowledged as Mr. Herbert Smiley Sr., and not just another Black man.

During the Great Depression in Mississippi, people of all kinds, Black, White, and Native American, would walk down what is now Mississippi State Route (SR) 15 with nothing. No food, water, shelter, and possibly not hope. When they would pass by my grandparents' farm, my grandmother would go into her kitchen and find whatever she could spare like fruit, nuts, jarred vegetables, or leftovers from the previous night's supper. Never mind the fact she and my grandfather had a house full of children to feed themselves. With a heartfelt prayer and message: "God bless you," she would send them on their way. This is what I call the Smiley-Butler-Moore Family's "DNA of humanity," and it still runs through our veins today.

My grandparents were not the Black family that worked for someone else, and their "work hard, self-sufficiency, help the less fortunate, and family first" mentality trickled down to my father, aunts, and uncles. My ancestors have always demonstrated tremendous generosity to their local community and were role models who showed up when a neighbor needed help, even if the neighbor did not look like them. They embraced the attitude of "helping someone" even while living in the Jim Crow era. Yet they chose to rise above it. For over fifty years, I have had the honor of witnessing my parents, uncles, aunts, brothers, sisters, cousins, my wife, and my daughter share God's blessings with others.

NEWTON, MISSISSIPPI, Circa 1950–

From 1951 to 1956, my dad served in the U.S. Army and was sent to fight in the Korean War. My parents met in their hometown of Newton Mississippi, and when my dad got out of the Army in 1956, he and my mother were part of the Great Migration to the north. That year they landed in Chicago, Illinois.

In 1956, my parents joined the Great Migration from the South. Historians suggest that between 1910 and 1970, over six million African Americans went from places in the South like Louisiana, Mississippi, Missouri, and Arkansas to urban centers in the North, like Chicago, Detroit, and Flint.[3] In fact, a blue-collar wage in the urban North was about three times as much as African Americans could earn in the rural South.[4]

The courage, perseverance, and faith my father, mother,

aunts, and uncles demonstrated was life changing. Not only for them, but for future generations of Smileys. And when it comes to education, I am proud to say my parents were high school graduates.

History shows secondary education was not a real or safe option in Mississippi during the 1950's through the 1960's. After settling in the northern cities, my parents knew the next step in the American dream was to own a home. A high school diploma and some college courses afforded a couple of my uncles General Motors (GM) mechanic and assembly line jobs, and support from the local Teamster union. At the time, American auto industry jobs paid good money and had great benefits, but they were tough to get.

Two of my uncles (Herbert Jr. (HB) and David Smiley), worked for GM in Flint, Michigan. Their salaries pushed them into what we call today "the middle-class," and with the money they made they were on a path to owning a home and having a solid retirement plan.

When my mom, dad, and my three older siblings, left Mississippi, they were headed to Flint so my dad could join my uncles working at the GM plant there. However, unbeknownst to them, God had a different plan.

While visiting his siblings in Chicago, my dad's car broke down. At that time, he couldn't afford the needed repairs to continue driving to Flint. How could the car break down at such a wrong time, and in the wrong place? But my parents shrugged it off and said, "Well, I guess we're going to stay in Chicago," and that is how the Glover Smiley, Sr. chapter in Chicago, Illinois began.

God's plan worked out wonderfully in Chicago. My father

got a union job at a company called Continental Coffee located near the Chicago River northside. His company was not only a major distributor of coffee, but Continental also distributed a ton of restaurant and hotel food supplies. Everything from sugar, pancake mix, spices, sugar, jellies, and coffee creamers. A good thing about working for a restaurant and hotel supplier is the employees received a nice discount at the company store. Needless to say, our panty at home was well stocked with everything Continental Coffee offered at discount prices to their employees.

Aside from his union steward job at Continental, my father went back to school, and got his barber's license while working a fulltime job. His side gig as a licensed barber was instrumental and helped the family stay on sound financial ground. Yes, there were a few lean times while growing up, but my parents always found a way to make ends meet. Yes, arduous work and sacrifice will pay off. Looking forward, my dad knew being a barber would come in handy for a family with eight boys!

The rest of the plan that was supposed to happen in Flint worked out just as well in Chicago. My family's move to Chicago was during the start of the Civil Rights movement, and although most of the media focus was on the South, tension was rapidly building in the big cities in the North.

During this time in American history, the respected social standing for the African American man was centered around two implied factors. One, being a Veteran, and two, do you own a home? Smiley Family report? Check and check.

The Smiley's who migrated to the North all bought homes, established relationships in their respective neighbors, and established foundational roots for future generations. While it was not easy, there was only one way forward for them back then. It was all part of God's plan, and everything happened at the right place at the right time.

ARIZONA, 2022–

When I sat down to write the *Smiley Leadership and Mentoring Experience*, I was overwhelmed with gratitude as I recounted my family's legacy, and how it shines through what we built at Sonoran Technology. We built a company that strives to be the best place people have ever worked. This book outlines the leadership principles we used to build such a business. You can apply it to yourself personally, professionally, and organizationally.

Our team members each have their own plan they will no doubt live out. As small business owners and leaders, we are entrusted with the responsibility of helping them live their plan, but in order to do that, we must understand our plan first. Much of that starts with our history, and the people and experiences that shaped us—even from generations ago.

Ask yourself: who and what was in your plan at the right place and right time? Why were those people and experiences there? How did they lead you here?

I thought about the July 1971 shooting that took place at the summer little league baseball game. When I ran home, I ran to my father, even past the local firehouse. Why?

Because I knew the role my father played in my life. To me, my father was Superman. When I left the nest at 18 years old to join the Air Force, I realized Superman was real, but he did not wear a red cape with a big "S" on his chest. No, the real Superman lived on Troy Street and wore a khaki shirt with a Continental

Coffee Company logo. The real Superman was six-foot-one, 190 pounds, raised ten kids, and worked as many jobs as necessary to take care of his family. My real-life Superman fixed the furnace in February, leaky faucets, broken windows, and put a new roof on the house himself!

This Superman was a father to my friends who did not have a father. When tough times knocked at Smiley's front door, the Superman I lived with was steadfast, defiant, and humble all at once. Our father made Christmas miracles happen year after year, sacrificing more than anyone could possibly imagine. Glover L. Smiley, Sr., was an exceptional role model, father, husband, friend, protector, and God-loving man who will be missed but never forgotten.

That is why I ran to my father.

My father, mother, and my Aunt Myrtie Moore had a lot to do with shaping me to into the leader and mentor I am today—a leader that strives to be fair, honest, respectful, humble, focused, philanthropic and encouraging. Before I forget, and so that you know, I am a man with flaws and some regrets. Now, I look forward to passing on what I have learned to you, and empower you to embrace your heroes, and become a force for your family, for your community, for your company, and for your faith. Finally, I sincerely hope this book is not a one-time read for you. Rather, that it becomes a life-long reference in your personal library. As such, at the end of each chapter you find a list of chapter takeaways that reminds you of the salient points for your immediate use. Let's get to work.

CHAPTER 0 TAKEAWAYS

- God has a plan, and everything happens right on time.

- As leaders, we are entrusted with the responsibility of helping others.

- Embrace the virtues of family, teamwork, resilience, and humility.

- Your story and your journey have value.

CHAPTER 1

Life Change (Purpose, Passion, and Fear)

Why I Went into Business

It's exciting to be a part of something brand new (children, marriage, relationships, entrepreneurship, etc.) and other experiences that last a lifetime. When you're there at the beginning, there are a ton of emotions: excitement, anticipation, optimism, anxiety, and, of course, uncertainty.

I have only been a part of something brand new four times in my life. First was my marriage to Malinda. Second was the birth of my daughter, Rachel. Third was the first day I went to the very first service at Palm Valley Church in Goodyear, Arizona. Fourth was the first day the doors opened at Sonoran Technology.

Here is what I think will resonate with other leaders: The times I was there on the first day of a new beginning have served me very well. My experience over time at Palm Valley Church, for example, helped reveal my new purpose during a new season in my life (i.e., life after the Air Force).

I found my purpose through prayer and by talking to people I trust. Oftentimes we ask ourselves, "Why didn't I know my purpose when I was younger?" The truth is that maybe if I knew it when I was younger, I could have screwed it up. A good friend once told me, "Be careful you don't let your talents take you to a place your character can't handle."

The question that I struggled with early on was, "Will God ever give me more than I can handle? Will He reveal His purpose for my life when I'm ready or when He's ready?" Rick Warren's book *The Purpose Driven Life* outlines five different purposes we all have: to worship, to unselfishly love fellow members of God's family, to assume Jesus's values and character, to serve others, and to spread God's love through your unique mission.[5] My time at Palm Valley Church provided me clarity on my unique mission.

My family and I started attending Palm Valley Church on October 1, 2000. The church had a simple message: "At Palm Valley, we take Jesus seriously but not ourselves. We believe in having fun, and we also believe church should not be boring."[6] Back then we met in the Palm Valley Cinemas—that's right, a local movie theater. During the first five years, the church grew from an intimate group into a multicampus church serving over 5,000 people on the weekends. During the early years, I knew most of the congregation's names and recognized most of the people at church. After serving on the trustee board for about three years, I decided to leave the board in order to bring in some new and fresh talent, new ideas, and some new energy.

Around 2007 I met with one of the young pastors. His name is Darius. He is very smart, intelligent, witty, and full of passion. Although Darius was probably young enough to be my son, I always referred to him as one of the pastors on staff. I told Darius, "I've lost my way. No, not as a Christian, but I've lost my purpose in this church because it's gotten so big."

"Well, I think you should pray about it, and I'll do the same," he said.

Maybe you've been in a situation similar to the one I was experiencing when it comes to rediscovering or discovering your purpose. I took Darius's advice.

I talked with Malinda, prayed about it, went back to God, and discovered my purpose, or my "unique mission," as Pastor Rick Warren would call it; to spread God's love by providing positive life change to myself, my peers, and my community. Unbeknownst to me at the time, that purpose became Sonoran Technology.

If I learned anything from evaluating my own family history and those "wrong place, wrong time" moments, it was that the plans I have for myself do not always follow the plan God has. Personal life events will influence our professional aspirations, and if we embrace these professional changes with the right frame of mind, they can lead to life change.

Earlier in my post-air force career, I was working at a company where my Air Force knowledge and leadership was an advantage. Before taking the job, I told them that my wife and I were planning on making Arizona our next home. I wanted to be clear that we did not want to move back to the Washington, DC, area.

"Not a problem," they said. The CEO and vice president of my soon-to-be new employer told me I could work from home in Arizona and then come to DC once a month for staff meetings to see and meet with corporate staff members. To me, this was an ideal scenario—a scene that is being played out twenty years later in the post-COVID-19 work environment.

When I started working, I hit the ground running. My education and Air Force leadership, command, operations training, and combat experience in Operation DESERT STORM uniquely qualified me to start in a midlevel executive position in the company.

The company leadership structure included the CEO, president, several vice presidents, directors, program managers, and then front-line professionals. Starting at the director level, I went on to grow my operations training division to over 100 people in three years. I was on this meteoric path as a director and earned the admiration and appreciation of my bosses.

Then at the beginning of the third year there was a leadership change. I didn't know it then, but that new leadership was going to help me, one way or another, make a great change in my own professional life. The signs of what was about to come were there; I just had not noticed. Funny thing about real life: there is no scary music that warns you something bad is about to happen. In hindsight, things changed for a couple of reasons.

First, I was still considered an outsider because I worked remotely. Second, a few of my peers who had seniority thought I did not have the credentials, even though the past leadership knew I did. Third, and probably the most obvious to everyone other than me, I was not part of "the group."

Today, the former leadership of that company are still good friends of mine. Our relationship from day one was based on respect, integrity, loyalty, and trust. Turns out that trust and integrity are not always present in today's corporate America. Truth be told, I did not adequately prepare myself for this new culture I was about to enter during my transition from the military. I did not spend enough time on understanding how corporate America functions behind closed doors. Bottom line: I was naive to life outside of the military culture. Years later I came across a quote by Mark Twain that put that experience into perspective.

"It ain't what you don't know that gets you into trouble. It's what you know for sure that just isn't so."[7]

The new leadership showed me that it was time for a change.

A three-year run of skyrocketing as a corporate director came to a screeching halt. I found myself at the end of the runway with no speed brake and absolutely no idea of what was next for my life.

Now I could have thrown a pity party, but I did not. I called Malinda, told her it was time to find a new professional path, and I went to the movies. Yes, the movies! The movies are how I escape and put the world on hold for a few hours while I collect myself.

A month later, I came across the book *God Is My CEO: Following God's Principles in a Bottom-Line World* by Larry Julian, and I told myself, "I don't ever want this situation to happen again."

That's when I seriously began to think about starting a small business. My purpose, the unique mission I had discovered at Palm Valley Church, resurfaced to create life change for myself and others. To do that, I needed to take as much control of the decisions in my life as I could.

I left the toxic pond and jumped into a body of fresh water to be in business for something bigger than myself. In this new water, the culture was better, and it wasn't full of sharks. Better yet, the new water was infinite, and I could grow to be whatever size fish I wanted to be.

I started an entirely different path for myself. The new path was clear, like a blank canvas, and I jumped in with confidence and very little fear of failure. Does this sound familiar to you?

I took everything I learned in my career—the good, bad, and the ugly—with me to Sonoran Technology.

While I was skilled and experienced in leadership and military aviation and operations training, I'm grateful for my past experiences for what they taught me about business and understanding the corporate work culture. It wasn't some cautionary tale about working for a wayward company; it was the golden nuggets I was able to take away from a *painful experience* that pushed me forward.

As I read *God Is my CEO* (which I highly recommend), it reassured me that I could do this.[8] I called a few of my friends who had previously worked for me and told them, "It's time to move on, and if you want to go with me, come on and be a part of something new and exciting."

The first person I called was Pete Ehrenfeld, a retired Air Force Master Sergeant and former military recruiter. Pete and I met while working for my former employer. I said, "Pete, we're going to start our own company and I just need you to help me get it off the ground in terms of recruiting." So, Pete Ehrenfeld and his wife, Patricia, came over to the house and I shared with them what I had in mind. They both agreed Pete would join the company as part owner. Through Sonoran Technology, I told Pete the plan was to create positive life change for anyone who became part of the Sonoran Family.

I'm not sure if it was an accident, or divine intervention that set both Peter and me on this soon to be life-changing journey: starting a new small business. Nonetheless, it was clear that God was providing me a new path, one where I could spread His love through a new and clearly defined mission of creating life change. Have any personal obstacles pushed you into a new professional sphere?

New Beginnings

Starting a new business is risky and it is not for the faint-hearted!

Statistically, according to the Bureau of Labor Statistics, about 20% of new businesses fail in the first year, 50% fail in the first five years, and 70% of small businesses fail in the first ten years.[9] Would you jump out of an airplane if there was a 70% chance the parachute would not open? Or 50%? Even just 20%? Absolutely not.

In all of the excitement, Pete and I had to look past fear because in the end, this life change we were seeking was worth the risk. Finally, the most satisfying part of this new journey was the only one I had to report and answer to was God.

When I retired as a lieutenant colonel in 2002, I had some money saved up and also had my Air Force retirement pension my family could rely on. On the surface, it might not seem like much. However, it was a great safety net to have, which simply meant my family had a roof over their heads, and we weren't going to go hungry. With Malinda working as a nurse, our family savings, and our Air Force retirement, we had our financial parachute. As new business owners, Pete and I had a few advantages that aided in our growth and success. Pete and I had the advantage of having led people during our Air Force careers. We knew how to plan, organize, execute, and communicate. Bottom line, we had an **experience advantage** that helped us to build a strategic-focused purpose driven business plan. What advantages do/did you have?

Another parachute we had was relying on our boss, God, who is perfect. Whenever I'm in question, I turn to God and ask for guidance and wisdom. As small business owners, we normally do not answer to anybody within the organization, so it helps tremendously to answer to a divine influence on the often-lonely leadership journey.

It's safe to say that from the very first day of becoming a small business owner, my military planning experiences have served me well. My advice: always have a primary plan and a backup plan. I have been known to have a backup plan for the backup, if necessary, just because things change in business just like they change in the fog of war. The fog of small business ownership isn't that much different. I think everyone should consider having a back-up, so you are not caught by surprise.

It's been said that planning comes from experience, which comes from failure. A countless number of critical thinkers have said during some point in their professional careers, "wow, that didn't work out like I thought it was going to work out." An effective leader and mentor must learn from and take advantage of each and every experience because experience helps develop foresight. When I sat down to develop the plan to launch Sonoran Technology, we purposely built in several employment options just in case things did not work out. Just like Tom Hanks said in the movie *A League of Their Own,* "if it was easy, anybody would do it."[10] If you have a clear purpose going into business rely on that, and the rest of the plan usually falls in line.

The Reason for the Business

Starting a new business during the Great Recession (Dec 2007-Aug 2009) was **emphatically** crazy. According to an October 2019 CNBC report, small business bankruptcies rose

74% during the Great Recession, with more than one million cases filed in federal courts in 2009.[11]

Fortunately for me I had my purpose to rely on. That purpose for starting a small business became clearer: To use Sonoran Technology as a medium to share my story of life change with other people. This was how I could be in charge of the decisions made for my life, and to make sure that the trauma experienced when I joined corporate America would never, ever, happen again.

Fully embracing this unique mission of creating life change, I molded it into a successful business model. It was important I did this in a not "in-your-face" way, but so that our employees could understand who I am, what I stand for, that I have flaws and blind spots, and that my faith will guide me as I lead this company.

Today, I feel comfortable expressing my faith when the situation dictates. Oftentimes when we are dining out as a team, it is very commonplace for someone to ask to pray before a meal.

This is one small instance, to ask for a blessing shows that our employees feel comfortable expressing who they are, and I encourage it. Notice I use the word faith, not religion because the two can have different interpretations. Bottom line, it has been my experience that no one has ever confronted me on my faith. Also, I purposely do not use the title CEO, rather, I am the president of Sonoran Technology. What a humbling and unbelievable experience to say that I report to no one on this planet because God is my CEO.

It's important to understand, no matter how much you plan (like Peter and I did when we started the company during the Great Recession), there comes a point in time when you realize that you are not in control. What do you have control over? The weather? No. The bank approving your loan request? No.

Whether an employee stays or quits? No. We only have control over the decisions we make. I believe God gives us free will to make decisions and search for meaning. We have no control over what people want to say or do to us. We have no control over getting a pay raise, or over the Great Recession.

The only thing we can control is how we respond. Peter and I, as leaders, decided we were going to respond by going into business to follow our purposes.

Why did **you** go into business?

If you haven't already done so, here is an opportunity to write down why you went into business:

a. _____

b. _____

c. _____

It doesn't matter how many reasons you have for going into business, the point is, you unequivocally know why.

I would not recommend you go into business if the number one reason is to simply make money. Yes, making money, operating "in the black" is vitally important. If you are not making money, it is just a hobby (more on that later). Your purpose for going into business should guide your future decisions, and if your number one reason you went into business was to make money, you will find yourself making money decisions and not business decisions, which is oftentimes a recipe for disaster.

Because Sonoran Technology's purpose and reason for going into business was to create life change, I don't make money decisions. Rather, our leadership team focuses on making business and people decisions.

Ultimately, your purpose will help define how you measure success, the infrastructure you build, the customers you engage, and the people you impact. Finding, and then following your purpose is the first step in the ***Smiley Leadership and Mentoring Experience.*** The other steps on your small business journey should involve metrics, defining your unique leadership style, taking care of people, having the right infrastructure (i.e., tools and resources), consistently engaging your employees, improving customer satisfaction, observing the competition, valuing the struggle, and embracing humility.

> *Finding, and then following, your purpose is the first step in the Smiley Mentoring Leadership and Mentoring Experience*

This book is a collection of my personal stories and professional experiences as a small business owner, leader, and mentor. Hopefully this book will help you on your journey toward becoming a level five leader, enhancing your life, your peers, your followers, and your community. This book is not a prescriptive how-to start, build, or run a small business book. Rather, it is designed to help you understand and implement a host of small business, leadership, and mentoring principles in your own way that will help you to change your life and others. Enjoy the journey!

CHAPTER 1 TAKEAWAYS

- The *Purpose Driven Life* outlines five different purposes we all have: to worship, to unselfishly love fellow members of God's family, to assume Jesus' values and character, to serve others, and to spread God's love through your unique mission.

- Starting a new business is risky and it is not for the faint-hearted!

- Avoid making purely money decisions. Focus on making smart business and people decisions.

CHAPTER 2

Measuring Success

Developing an Infrastructure for Success

Before I went into the Air Force, I was a musician. I played the trombone and taught myself how to play the piano years later. In high school, I was in the concert band and the newly formed school jazz band. These are the guys I spent most of my time together with during and after school. Not everyone took being in the jazz band seriously. The ones that did were the guys who showed up at 6:30am because our band director, Mr. Strickland told us, "Serious musicians do what is necessary to be great at their craft." Eventually, my friends and I formed an R&B band and called ourselves the *Cook County Express*. Without question, at least in my mind, we were set on becoming the next *Earth, Wind, and Fire*, or *Cool and the Gang*, or *Tower of Power* band.

When the band first started I was not the obvious leader—no one was. Everyone in the band was musically and vocally talented, which was a big plus for a group of amateurs. Even though we never decided who would be the leader, for some unknown reason, the leadership role landed in my lap. Genuine leaders rise up as various situations present themselves. Maybe it's because of their style, charisma, intellect, the ability to find solutions, or because they are the ones who understand the situation and who see the big picture. As natural born leaders, they simply get things done, and they inspire others to willingly follow them.

During my last two years of college at Northeastern Illinois University and the Air Force Reserve Officer Training (ROTC) detachment at Illinois Institute of Technology in Chicago, I got back with the band. I told myself, "If the band gets a break and takes off, I am going to turn down a commission as an Air Force officer." That was my plan and I reluctantly shared it with my father. Back then, being a successful musician did not seem like a long shot. In reality, it was more like a moon shot.

No matter how hard we chase our dreams, for me, the dream of being in a superstar band did not work out. That is when I realized my passion at the time, (music) was clashing with my life purpose. Though my true purpose was yet to be revealed to me, I had new clarity that my purpose was not the life of a musician. For me, that passion for being the next superstar musician and God's purpose clashed.

When your passion and God's purpose clash, God is going to win out every time. It was as if God knocked on my head and said, "Hello, you are a cadet in the Air Force ROTC program! You gave the band two years, and it's not going to happen. You are going to be an Air Force officer! Hello? Are you listening to Me?"

Getting that spiritual nudge made a huge difference in my life journey. The reward was when I accepted God had specific plan for my life. The voice clearly said, "Hey, I know your passion, but that's not what I have planned for you, that's not your purpose." Had I ignored that knock on my head and decided to become a musician, all the things that I am happy about in my life would not have happened. I would not have met my wife, have an amazing daughter, or who knows what else. Just like the movie *Back to the Future*, you change one event in your life, and the whole outcome changes.

With that divine intervention, I had to redefine what success meant to me. It was no longer becoming a professional musician. All of these things happened before my purpose was fully revealed: to create life change for myself and others. I had to set that dream aside.

Tough decisions are part of life. Some people are comfortable and confident when it comes to making challenging decisions. And for others, making tough decisions can be like going to the dentist. Then there are those who simply refuse to "make the call" and leave the decision up to someone else. Making tough decisions, right, wrong, or indifferent, makes us accountable, responsible, and experienced. My trusted friend Dan G has a quote at the bottom of his email signature block that reads, "I am the CEO of Myself." Hopefully, you have already experienced the inevitable "passion versus purpose clash." Good for you. The results of the clash will give you a metric for measuring success. Bottom line, never let someone else define what success looks and feels like for you.

As a small business owner/entrepreneur, defining what success looks like for you and your business is the second step in the *Smiley Leadership Mentoring Experience.* When we define how we measure success, we can focus on building the necessary infrastructure that supports your business.

In 2012, retired General and former United States Secretary of State Colin Powell gave a Technology, Entertainment and Design (TED) talk titled *Kids Need Structure.* His talk is relevant to us as business leaders because it helps us understand the structure we come from, which helps reveal who we are, and what we value as leaders. General Powell also reminds us that it does not depend on where you start in life, it is what you do with your life that counts. We all have different advantages that make us unique. Where we start in life has a direct connection to how we define success. Understanding the advantages, we have had in our journey will make us better leaders and mentors.

General Powell explains:

> *"...The gift of a good start. Every child ought to have a good start in life ... I was privileged to have that kind of good start. I was not a great student. I was a public-school kid in New York City, and I did not do well at all. I have my entire New York City Board of Education transcript from kindergarten through college. I wanted it when I was writing my first book. I wanted to see if my memory was correct, and, my God, it was. Straight C everywhere. And I finally bounced through high school, got into the City College of New York with a 78.3 average, which I should not have been allowed in with, and then I started out in engineering, and that only lasted six months. And then I went into geology, 'rocks for jocks.' This is easy. And then I found ROTC. I found something that I did well and something that I loved doing, and I found a group of youngsters like me who felt the same way. So, my whole life then was dedicated to ROTC and the military. I say to young kids everywhere, as you're growing up and as this structure is being*

developed inside of you, always be looking for that which you do well and that which you love doing, and when you find those two things together, man, you got it. I tell young people everywhere, whenever the opportunity presents itself, it is not where you start in life, it is what you do with your life that determines where you end up in life. I tell them it is only an opportunity if you are prepared and ready. I tell them you cannot be satisfied with getting ready, you have to be ready, and always believe in yourself."[12]

Every now and then I get asked, "what are the keys to success?" My answer back then was a list of things you needed to do. That all changed when I heard General Powell's viewpoint. Reflecting on my life journey, I realized the gift of having a good start is a blessing, a gift that should not be taken for granted, ever. A loving family that supported and believed in me, and a mother and father who instilled in me the need to be disciplined, respectful, trustworthy, and accountable were critical.

A community where neighbors looked out for one another, and the structure the Air Force afforded me, were also important. All of these experiences are part of my life journey. They are part of the reason I made the leap of faith into the small business world: to help change my own life and the lives of others.

As business owners, we speak on behalf of an entire company, not just ourselves. So, while we have our own personal purpose, having a well-defined moral purpose for your business (i.e., the values that guide your decision making) is equally important. Your business moral purpose is different than the vision and mission statement. While those are both necessary, there will times when you will be challenged with moral and ethical decisions. To effectively address those issues, having a moral purpose for the business will serve as a decision-making guide for you and your employees. Sonoran Technology's moral purpose is ***"with dignity, respect, and kindness, improve the quality of life for everyone we encounter."***

Your company's moral purpose will help you and your team make smart moral and ethical decisions (e.g., making business decisions instead of money decisions). That moral purpose will also have a direct impact on your company's success.

At Sonoran Technology, our moral purpose proved to be invaluable in guiding us toward our strategic goals. Sonoran Technology's moral purpose holds us accountable to create a workplace where people are treated with dignity, respect, and that people are cared for—which we demonstrate with employee pay, benefits, safety, and morale. As such, we measure and define our success two ways:

1. When an employee leaves the company, do they say, "This is the best company I have ever worked for!"?
2. Did we keep our promise of a business that puts people before profit?

A moral purpose is a great first step in designing the company infrastructure and the culture designed for long-term success. As our definition of success changes over time, we must also change the infrastructure required to support our goals and business strategy.

Is Your Business Profitable?

If your business is not making money, you may want to consider it a hobby, not a business. I have plenty of friends who have wonderful hobbies that bring them joy. Personally, I don't know anyone that depends on their hobby for making a living. However, if you are making a living with your hobby, please share your secret because you are amazingly blessed.

A business that is making money is not the same as a business that is profitable. I often hear business owners referring to their annual revenue. But, if your cost of doing business exceeds your revenue, then you are not profitable; you're losing money. One way we measure financial success at Sonoran Technology is simple: Are we in the black? In other words, is the company making a profit? Believe me, banks only know two financial colors, black and red. Red is always bad! In the early years of Sonoran Technology, around 2009, I would ask my chief financial officer, "Are we in the black?" She said, "Yes, we're in the black by $200." Yes! I was ecstatic because I knew this would make my local bank president happy. My first banking experience was with a brilliant woman named Candace who was the president of a local small community bank. Candace was the first person who taught me the "Five Cs" of banking: character, capacity, capital, collateral, and conditions.

1. *Character: Refers to the borrower's reputation and willingness to repay the loan.*
2. *Capacity (Cash Flow): Refers to the borrower's ability to repay the loan based on their income and financial obligations.*

3. *Capital: Refers to the borrower's net worth or financial resources that can be used as collateral or as a source of repayment.*

4. *Collateral: Refers to the borrower's assets that can be pledged as security for the loan.*

5. *Conditions: Refers to the economic and industry conditions that may affect the borrower's ability to repay the loan.*

Candace's lesson on being "bankable" was priceless because the economy was mired in the Great Recession and the banking community was on high alert. The good thing for me was that I already knew Candace before I began banking with her. We had previously attended several small business and economic summits in the local community and had formed a great relationship.

Having a clear understanding of what the banking industry was going through and their view of all businesses, big and small, boiled down to this: every business has the same last name, and that last name is *Risk*! However, it is the first name of the business that is the most important. That name falls into three categories: low, medium, and high. If your profit and loss (P&L) statement shows you are consistently in the black, cash flow is steady, and you have collateral, chances are you fall into the category of being Low Risk, which means you are bankable.

If you recall, starting around 2008 through 2011, people were losing their homes, which for a lot of small business owners was their main source of collateral for the banks. Finally, if you have never heard the phrase "character counts," believe me, it does. Candace shared with me that the only reason she took a chance with me (giving Sonoran our first line of credit) is that she "believed in [my] business plan, knew [me] to be trustworthy, and a person of high character—" all of that meaning I had earned her trust.

Another way we ensured the company was profitable during the early years is I did not take a salary for the first year. Business owners have to make huge sacrifices if they are truly committed to making their business work. Pete and I were committed to making Sonoran work. We used all of our military leadership experiences to plan ahead, methodically solve problems, build strong relationships, and ensure our employees got paid first. Effective business owners get paid last, always. This is why having some kind of financial parachute is so important when you decide to take a leap of faith and start a small business.

A clear, concise, and realistic financial metric of success should guide your overall strategic plan. Hopefully, you have a strategic plan for growth and a path to profitability. That has to be part of your big picture. As long as you're not losing money and the bills are being paid, you're already on the path to financial success and creating a life change for the people that work with you. The next step is to grow that success, and to increase the impact in the marketplace your business serves.

Sonoran Technology's Line of Business

Now, let me give you some context as to what we do as a business so you can better understand how we fulfill our purpose of providing life change to those we work with and our impact on the marketplace we serve.

At Sonoran we primarily train Pilots, Weapons System Officers (WSOs), Air Battle Managers (ABMs) and other aircrew specialists in how to fly and operate complicated aircraft systems.

Different weapon systems we have trained currently (and in the past) include the E-3 Airborne Warning and Control System (AWACS) aircraft, the B-1, B-2, B-52, F-16, RC/OC-135, and the ground-based Command and Control (C2) units just to name a few. We contract with various military branches (e.g., the Air Force, Navy, Army) within the Department of Defense.

Most of our training is conducted in the classroom and in aircraft simulators of various airplanes. Additionally, Sonoran provides a host of squadron-level operational support services such as aircrew scheduling, training operations, logistics, training evaluations, and administrative functions. Our impact on mission-essential support functions allows our military customers to focus on live flight operations.

During my Air Force career, I was not a pilot. I was an aircrew member and Master Air Battle Manager qualified as a Mission Crew Commander (MCC), Senior Director, and Weapons Director on the E-3 AWACS aircraft. As the MCC, the Aircraft Commander (pilot) and I were responsible for a crew of 18-24 mission specialists. We are running the entire air war from the E-3 jet. Our mission crew specialists are communicating to every airplane that is flying under our control, airmen on the ground integrated with an Army unit, and the senior military leaders located in the Air Operation Center (AOC). As the senior airborne battle management and command and control element, E-3 crews coordinate and make real time combat engagement decisions such as clearance to shoot, search and rescue efforts of a downed aircraft, airborne refueling, and just everything you can think of during combat air operations. During Operation DESERT STORM, it was not unusual to have hundreds of multinational aircraft flying at any given time.

My Air Force career was the perfect training ground for becoming a highly reputable and experienced small business owner operating primarily in the aerospace industry as a defense contractor. The professional services that Sonoran provides is obtained by bidding on and winning competitive federal contracts.

This is where it all funnels back to Sonoran's strategic plan for growing the company. My team and I must ensure we have the infrastructure (accounting systems, security clearances, recruiting tools, contracting, subject matter expertise, and personnel) in order to execute and meet 100% of the contract requirements we signed up for with the federal government.

Question—is your business ready to perform the services or provide products you are selling? Do you have the resources, policies and procedures, people, finances, and infrastructure in place so you can start executing your strategic plan?

"The Best Place I've Ever Worked"

The other metric of success at our company is when people leave for whatever reason, they fervently say "Sonoran Technology was the best company I have ever worked for." This to me means first, the company took great care of our employees and their families. Second, we earned and kept their trust and did what we said we would do. Third, our company culture was one cemented in fairness, kindness, respectfulness, and accountability at all levels. Bottom line, over the past 17 years, we positively changed our employees' lives for the better. This is a leadership and mentoring method you can take to the bank.

Many Sonoran employees (approximately 80%) are military Veterans, so there is a myriad of reasons an employee could leave the company. They may leave because their spouse received an assignment to Korea, the spouse decides to stay home and care for the kids, or they have decided to retire and move on to the next chapter in their lives. During an employee's exit interview, if they say, "this was the best company I have ever worked for," that is real success in the eyes of Sonoran Technology. Their words tell us as a company, we did our very best in taking care of the employees by providing a friendly and fun workplace, giving the best salary benefits we could, and allowing them to balance work and family. If this is the kind of company you are running, chances are the company is getting the best and most from their employees. It also is a strong indicator your company's culture is on the right path to continued success and prosperity.

As you can see, there are two proven ways of measuring success: financial and relational. Often, these require different approaches as a business owner, mentor, and as a leader. There are people decisions, business decisions, and there are sometimes money decisions. Business decisions, as I define them, impact your employees, your customers, and your company's culture. Business decisions are decisions that will have a positive and moral impact much greater than the short-term or short-sighted money decision.

A smart and carefully thought-out business decision is for the benefit of everything associated with your business. Everyone is going to benefit from that—whether it is taking less profit, improving employee benefits, or terminating employees because the scope of the contract has decreased. Often, decisions like these have a big strategic effect on a business.

On the other hand, a money decision, like reducing employee benefits or pay in order to increase the company's profit margin, will have short term immediate benefits on the bottom line. Although that seemingly smart decision could deliver temporary or short-term financial benefits, the more likely results are employee dissatisfaction, fractured trust, a damaged culture, and ultimately, employees choosing to leave your company. My good friend Pastor Greg, rest in peace, was famous for saying, "people get funny when you mess with the money."

Can you identify business decisions and money decisions you have had to make? What were the results?

Commitment to Success

Now that you have outlined how you are going to measure success, you must make a commitment to accomplishing it.

Every business owner should ask themselves the following four questions:

1. *Is owning a business really what I want to do?*
2. *Do I have the energy and resources to see it through?*
3. *How do I know when to quit?*
4. *What will I do if I want to quit?*

I believe commitment falls into two categories for most small business owners when starting out: either you have a parachute, or you need to build a parachute. For example, I started Sonoran with a small financial parachute of personal savings and my military retirement pay. When I took the leap of faith, I committed to giving the company my all; 12, 14 hours a day, or whatever it took.

The second option is building your parachute as you go. Maybe you don't have any money saved up. You decide you are going to work a job and then you are going to run your business from 5:00pm to midnight as an example. You say goodnight to your spouse and the kids, and then it is off to work developing and running your dream business venture.

Either way, you must make a firm commitment (what I found out to mean unimaginable sacrifices) that you're in for the long haul. Just to be clear, there is nothing wrong with saying, "I got to have a side gig here because I have to pay the bills and I'm going to run my business on a part-time basis." If that is your reality, great. In fact, that is how a lot of great businesses were started! The difference is the more energy and time you spend developing your business, the chances are your business will experience profitable success sooner.

The world is full of people who think they are business owners. Whether you have a business or a hobby, a key factor in measuring growth is the amount of time you dedicate to it. The more time and effort you put in, the quicker you will see results. For example, the person who plays golf five days a week will probably be a much better golfer than the person who plays once a month, or like me, once a year. Being a business owner is not for the "faint hearted" or delicately committed. I cannot emphasize the virtue of "time commitment" enough for the new business owner. Equally important, if you are going to create life change for people, you must love what you're doing. It needs to be that unharnessed energy that gets you out of bed every morning. I have never met an extraordinarily successful person who hates what they do, have you?

There's a reason people use the phrase, "this is my baby" when referring to a special project or thing. Why? Because babies need constant care (e.g., time, feeding, and energy). Babies cannot do anything without the help, commitment, and support of someone else. For your baby business, that person is you and your team. Now, as it relates to making that transition into entrepreneurship and business, everybody has their own journey. Particularly, for Veterans. In 2008, the U.S. Small Business Administration (SBA) started a program called *Boots to Business* to help prepare veterans for business ownership once they leave or retire from the military. When a Veteran leaves the service, they leave the comfort, familiarity, and culture of the base or post and go out into a world that is inherently different from the one they are used to. When it comes to the business world, their challenges are tenfold. Life inside the military community is somewhat different than the civilian community. For example, I have always considered myself a "rule follower." When I retired from the Air Force, I had a tough time dealing with people who were "rule benders." From my perspective if you are bending the rules, you are not following the rules.

This is an important distinction because it is the foundation of organizational culture, a topic I will discuss later. In the military there is a decorum and culture of respect and brotherhood/ sisterhood inside the walls of the military installation. But once you get outside the base gates, some Veterans aren't prepared for the difference.

Oftentimes those who leave the military may change jobs two or three times because it was not the right fit for them. Maybe they couldn't adopt the civilian world culture, or the job's pay and healthcare benefits were not comparable to what they were receiving in the military. Interestingly enough, according to the Bureau of Labor Statistics, Veterans are less likely to change jobs compared to non-veterans. In 2019, veterans had a job tenure of 3.5 years, while non-veterans had a job tenure of 3.3 years.[13] Leaving jobs is not a veteran specific issue, rather a societal workforce issue of employees committing to companies, and companies reciprocating that commitment. Creating "life change" and the "best company our employees have ever worked for" cuts down on turnover. Employee commitment starts with you, the leader.

I think it's worth mentioning again, we started Sonoran Technology in 2007, at the beginning of the Great Recession, and we had limited access to capital, but we kept growing one small contract at a time. We put our employees before profit, and we did not cut any of our overhead staff. Each time we got a new contract, we hired a new program manager to run it. As we continued to grow, we doubled down on commitment to our employees by offering medical benefits although it was not required by law. We made a point of visiting each out of state work location several times a year. Our employees knew all these things cost the company extra money. Our leadership actions resulted in high retention numbers and our employees' commitment to Sonoran.

The first thing each new hire recognizes is that Sonoran's company culture is a little different from their previous employer. For all of our Arizona-based employees, our corporate staff have the benefit of getting to know them on a personal level. From a cultural point of view, every employee is part of the Sonoran Family. We have social events such as chili-cookoffs, Veterans Day celebrations, and great Christmas parties. Our office staff take donuts and lunch to their work locations. Still today, every employee, regardless of their work location receives a hand-written birthday card from me, in addition to rewards that is part of our Employee Recognition Program, a huge morale booster.

Our company culture and commitment are always center stage because we believe in being there for our Sonoran Family members during the good and difficult times, as sickness, death, and just everyday hardships.

Prior to the COVID-19 pandemic, visiting our employees and customers across the country was standard operating procedures for our leadership team. At Christmas time, we have celebrations at all our operating locations. Our employees not only enjoy the camaraderie and fellowship, but they also look forward to it. Then the pandemic hit and all travel to the job sites momentarily ended. The first Christmas after the pandemic started, I asked my CFO, "how much money do we have set aside for Christmas parties this year?"

She said it was about $10,000 dollars including our corporate party. I met with the office staff and said, "go out and buy $50 gift cards, one for each of our employees in the field, and order special Christmas cards." The corporate staff members and I signed nearly 250 Christmas cards expressing our remorse that we could not celebrate in person as we had in the past. The message read: "We are so sorry, we cannot come out for the Christmas celebration, but we put this money aside, so please enjoy it. Take your wife, husband, girlfriend, boyfriend, partner out for lunch on us."

Shortly thereafter, our HR department received many calls and emails all saying the same thing—"Wow, we did not expect this! We worked for different companies, and they never did anything like this." This is just one small example of putting people over profit.

43

A highlight of my career as a business owner, and one of my favorites talking points for the **Smiley Leadership and Mentoring Experience** are the thank you letters and emails we received from our employees. I keep them on my desk as a reminder of what the company stands for and that what my staff and I are doing is making a difference in the lives of our employees and their families. Whenever possible, our Human Resources (HR) Manager visits or has virtual meetings with each worksite to explain current HR updates, particularly healthcare benefits.

As you can imagine, a lot of healthcare benefits are tied to federal legislation which is constantly changing. It gets confusing, but our HR team is available to connect with our employees and go over their benefits. This reminds me of a very special and heartfelt thank you letter I received from a former employee, Geno.

My wife Malinda and I went to Geno's retirement party after he left Sonoran. Geno is one of those guys you just connect with instantly. At his retirement party, I gave him a nice watch on behalf of Sonoran. We thanked Geno for his military service, his support on the previous Sonoran contract, and for being a great friend. He seemed a little surprised we took the time to go to his retirement party, but I was honored to even be invited! When Geno acknowledged me and our company during his speech, even though I was not his employer at the time, the guy who was his current employer seemed surprised. There was Geno, thanking his former employer, because that's how impactful Sonoran Technology was on his post-military civilian career. As business leaders, we can make a huge difference in someone's life. Your company's culture is your brand, and your brand, especially in the professional service industry, is one way to measure success.

One thing my team and I have learned in the federal contracting business is: *"contracts will end, but relationships with your employees, past and present will last forever if you do it right." -Paul Smiley*

How do you measure success?

Small Business 2.0 – Now What?

I want to close out this chapter with a short history lesson that a lot of small, medium, and large businesses experienced during the COVID-19 pandemic. It seemed like every time I turned on the news it was the same economic and financial forecast—"businesses are getting hammered, and the economy is on the edge of a global collapse." Not that the economic experts were wrong, or that people weren't losing their jobs, but no one seemed to offer any solutions or fixes, particularly for the small business community.

According to the U.S. Chamber of Commerce, small businesses (500 or fewer employees) make up 99.9% of all U.S. businesses.[14] As a small business owner, mentor, and deeply frustrated citizen, I began researching what was really happening in the small business world. The first move was to canvas some of the local small businesses in my local community (Goodyear, Avondale, Glendale, Surprise and Peoria, Arizona). By canvas, I mean get in the car and drive to some of these small businesses. I first started where I was a customer—restaurants, my barbershop, movie theaters, gyms, dry cleaners, the grocery store, etc. Some had closed for unknown reasons. Some of the local businesses had limited hours of operation, and too many businesses were victims of state ordinances (like operating restrictions) that stopped them from opening. For example, in July 2020, Arizona shut down all bars, gyms, water parks and movie theaters, just to name a few. After four months of research and deep thought, I put together a *Small Business 2.0* presentation targeted specifically to the small business community and asked this simple question: Now what?

Now that the pandemic restrictions are over, what lessons did we, as a country, learn? What was the small business owner's plan to get back into the game, should you decide to do so? Without a new plan, a plan that changes the way we think and operate as business owners, we are setting ourselves up for a repeat of the devastation COVID-19 had on the U.S. economy, and particularly the small business community.

With the help of the Arizona Department of Commerce, and the U.S. Small Business Administration's Arizona District Office, I was able to share the *Small Business 2.0: Now What?* presentation with hundreds of small business owners across the country.

In the presentation we discussed the future of small business, which I think is dependent on the type of market you are in, like the various categories listed below:

- Retail (except grocery & pharmacy)
- Travel / Transportation
- Employment Services
- Arts, entertainment, and recreation
- Accommodation and food services

During the pandemic, approximately 48% of workers were in occupations that required close physical proximity to their customers or co-workers, meaning their jobs could not be performed remotely.[15] This was a huge lesson for businesses in the market sectors previously mentioned. The challenge for the future is finding ways to stay operational during the next crisis, whether it's health or cyber related. For the United States, it all boils down to the fact we live in a "consumer-based" economy. When the spending stops, so does the U.S. economy.

Before COVID-19, a lot of businesses, both large and small, were on the "financial ropes" long before the pandemic arrived. In this case, their business plan was out of date or non-existent. They did not adapt to on-line buying services.

Some did not realize this simple truth: "if we don't take care of our customers, someone else will." Even today, there some small business owners who do not know their competition or understand that hiring the "right fit talent" is critical to success.

Meanwhile, profitable, and sustainable small businesses conduct customer surveys on a regular basis. When was the last time you conducted a check on your business? Let us begin with your customers. You can get to know your customers better by seeking post experience feedback. Here are a few questions you can ask:

- What makes our customers come back?
- What makes our customers take their business elsewhere?
- How do we communicate with our customers and how often?

For example, every time I have an interaction with Delta Airlines, whether it is a flight or talking to a customer service agent on the phone, within 48 hours they send me a short (heavy emphasis on short) survey asking for feedback. This helps build trust between me and the company, and the foundation for any relationship is trust. As small business owners, we realize that networking and relationships are NOT the same thing, but more on that later.

Another sure way to win over the competition and grow a loyal customer base is to under promise and over deliver. Make no mistake about it, in today's e-commerce purchasing environment, speedy delivery can earn your company customer loyalty.

Ultimately, what shapes a customer's perspective is their **personal experience** with your business and anyone associated with your business. This is a fact that should not be debated. Put on your consumer hat for a few minutes and think about the last ten businesses you interacted with as a customer. What was your experience; good, bad, or indifferent? Have you ever revisited a business where the experience was horrible? Have you ever recommended a family member or friend where your experience was disappointing? Now ask yourself, what was your response when your experience was great, or where the business exceeded your expectations? These customer experiences also apply to your small business. A customer's experience starts and ends with your company's culture and hiring the "right fit talent," with more on that in later chapters.

CHAPTER 2 TAKEAWAYS

- Defining what success looks like for you and your business is the second step in the *Smiley Leadership and Mentoring Experience*

- A business that is making money is not the same as a business that is profitable.

- There are two proven ways of measuring success: financial and relational. Often, these require different approaches as a business owner and as a leader.

- There are people decisions, business decisions, and there are money decisions.

- Every business owner should ask themselves four questions:

  1. Is this really what I want to do? Own a business!
  2. Do I have the energy and resources to see it through?
  3. How do I know when to quit?
  4. What will I do if I want to quit?

- Smart, and sustainable small businesses conduct customer surveys on a regular basis.

3   The Chocolate Cake Leader

As a leader, people are constantly watching you.

Whether it is leading a small business, a military unit, a sports team, or your family, people are looking for a reason to follow you. In this chapter, I'll explain what I believe makes a great "Chocolate Cake Leader" and excites others to follow you.

Today, some individuals have a clouded view of what authentic leadership is. People oftentimes have different views on what leadership means, what traits or characteristics makes a good leader, who can be a leader, who cannot, or the various leadership styles. The word "leadership" has gotten to the point academically where we need to create an agreeable understanding on the different types of leadership style that exist[16]:

- Authentic Leadership
- Servant Leadership
- Democratic Leadership
- Autocratic Leadership
- Laissez-faire Leadership
- Strategic Leadership

- Transformational Leadership
- Transactional Leadership
- Coach-Style Leadership
- Bureaucratic Leadership
- Toxic Leadership

This is a brief list of leadership types. What's important is that you have your own understanding of leadership and follow it to the best of your ability. Over the years, I have learned a lot of valuable leadership lessons. The one that come up all the time is really a question: "How do you know if you are an effective leader?"

How do we measure effective leadership? I found one answer to this question in the movie *Heart of Champions*. Coach Murphy, who is the new rowing coach at a fictitious Ivy league school, tells the beleaguered rowing team "leadership is measured in the hearts of those who follow..."[17] Wow, this blew me away the first time I heard it! As I mentioned earlier, how we see and value ourselves can be quite different from those around us. A question that I oftentimes ask is "how do you get to know the hearts of your true followers, not the ones pretending to follow you?"

I'm sure there are a lot of answers to this question, but **trust** is what comes to mind often. People who trust you are more likely to believe in you. As leaders, it is important that we demonstrate integrity, humility, honesty, truth, love, commitment, and character. Now character is the tricky one because it can be misconstrued to being perfect, which none of us are! Ever hear the term character flaws? Great! We all have them. A popular definition of character is the aggregate (total sum) of features and traits that form the individual nature of a person. If we are honest with ourselves, we know exactly what our flaws are, but that does not mean we are a bad person, or an ineffective leader. My last point on the topic of character deals with being truthful.

Manipulating the truth might be dismissed or used as an excuse in politics, (though it shouldn't be) but not in business. When I spoke to the 2023 graduating class at Arizona State University's New College, I told the graduating class, "Regardless of what anyone tells you, remember the truth never changes..." The benefits of being truthful with your followers cannot be overstated.

My personal definition of leadership is to inspire people to get things done, **willingly.** Special emphasis on the word willingly. Willing followers get the job done because they want to, not because they have to. These are the employees who can truly impact our personal and professional lives.

For example, anyone who joins our nation's armed forces has one thing in common: they must swear in by repeating the military oath of enlistment or military oath of office. The oath of enlistment is something that every service member must promise and adhere to for their entire military career. If you are entering as an officer, you will instead take the military oath of office.

As an officer, I took this oath:

> *"I, Paul Andrew Smiley, having been appointed an officer in the Air Force of the United States, as indicated above in the grade of 2nd Lieutenant, do solemnly swear (or affirm) that I will support and defend the Constitution of the United States against all enemies, foreign or domestic, that I will bear true faith and allegiance to the same; that I take this obligation freely, without any mental reservation or purpose of evasion; and that I will well and faithfully discharge the duties of the office upon which I am about to enter. So, help me God."*

As an officer, you have legitimate authority. This authority is to defend the Constitution of the United States. Very few people outside the military, except for elected officials, have that "legitimized authority." Legitimate authority means somebody created a legal hierarchy people agreed to participate in, and as a result, you agree to follow the person above you, even when you disagree.

However, in a small business, relying solely on legitimized power to lead, or to create that power over people so they will follow you, is not sustainable. Eventually, it will blow up in your face. If you can inspire them to follow you willingly, then you have created a sustainable and effective leadership environment.

Consider this football analogy in the 1998 NFL Entry Draft. Before the draft, there was much debate in the media on whether the Indianapolis Colts would select Peyton Manning or Ryan Leaf with the first overall pick. Both were considered excellent prospects and future franchise quarterbacks. Ryan Leaf was considered to have more upside and a stronger throwing arm, whereas Peyton Manning was considered a polished prospect who was NFL ready and more mature.

The Colts selected Manning and Leaf was selected second overall by the San Diego Chargers. Manning went on to be a five-time Most Valuable Player Award winner (the most of any player in NFL history), was a two-time Super Bowl champion, and was inducted into the Pro Football Hall of Fame in 2021. Meanwhile, Leaf was out of the NFL by 2002 and is considered one of the biggest draft busts in NFL history.

What was the difference between these two men and how they were so comparable once, and then ended up so drastically different? The answer was their leadership ability.

Word has it, the first thing Manning did when he landed in Indianapolis was tell the coaches something like "Give me the playbooks. Where are the playbooks? I must study." Conversely, it was said Leaf arrived in San Diego partying, got the big contract, and basked in his celebrity.

Manning went on to start 208 consecutive games and did not miss a game in his first thirteen seasons, another NFL record he holds. Then, in the 2011 season, he suffered what was considered a career changing neck injury and had to sit out the entire season. So where was Manning during that 2011 season (where the Colts ultimately went 2-14)? He was on the sidelines. That year the team went through four backup QBs. Each game, Manning was with each one of them, with his arm around him, mentoring, coaching and leading. While he was the starting QB, he was afforded some of that "legitimized power," yet instead he led by example and inspired the rest of the team to follow him willingly. It was arguable he could have won the MVP that season, without even playing.

True teamwork is inspirational. Teammates all push each other to be better and accountable. Sustainable leadership is not positionally based. Just because somebody is coaching a super-star athlete does not make them the leader of the team. Positions don't lead. People lead. Actions lead.

What actions are you taking to inspire your followers?

Metaphorically speaking, I consider myself a Chocolate Cake Leader. I see whatever project or task I am working on as a chocolate cake. In this scenario as a leader, our primary role is to provide our employees with all the ingredients and tools to bake a chocolate cake. How you get there is up to you.

If the team wants to use self-rising flour, skim, or whole milk, two eggs versus three eggs, butter or margarine, Betty Crocker, or Duncan Hines chocolate frosting, I'm ok with that. With respect to the tools, my job is to provide an oven, which in this setting is a well-tuned friendly and professional work environment. I consider Sonoran Technology a chocolate cake of all sorts. I love sharing this cake with our employees, business associates, our friends, my family, and our community. Collectively, we have all the ingredients needed, the "right fit talent," policies and procedures, infrastructure, financial resources, professional culture, and of course, our customers to make the cake. Our business plan is our recipe. The culture creates the right (or wrong) temperature. If the culture is wrong the cake will be raw, or worse yet, burned.

Here is the significant difference between a successful leader and an effective leader. The successful leader could say "thanks, this is a great looking chocolate cake, and it tastes so good." The effective leader says "excellent job, the cake is just what I expected. It looks great, let us all taste and enjoy it together."

The key here is teamwork. Take all the ingredients of a chocolate cake and put them on a table separately. Then, if you can stomach it, taste each one individually. Horrible right?

Eating a tablespoon of butter, sugar, salt, eggs, and flour by itself isn't good. As individuals, we are building our own chocolate cake too; what does our life amount to when we are done? I believe God has given each of us the ingredients we need, but it is up to us to put them together and bake the cake. Consider a two-oven scenario. One oven represents the company culture you're building as a business owner, while the other oven represents the faith you're building as an individual. The Bible in its truest sense is a plan; it is a recipe for making a cake out of your life.

This is a perfect plan, too. Yet we do not expect perfection because I, as an ingredient, am not perfect. My cake, your cake, any cake made by human beings is going to have a few lumps in it—that's life!

The biblical principles of trust, humility, selflessness, and sacrifice, all take time to develop. There are no shortcuts. Mistakes and missteps in our life take time to remove from our cake too. If you cracked the egg for your cake, shells got into the batter, and you didn't fish them out—when you share your cake with your friends and family, they are going to bite into eggshells. This is because you didn't take the time to remove the shells when they were first the problem. We must take the necessary time to work on the life we are building to have it taste right.

There is no such thing as a perfect cake. Yet, if we put faith in the perfect recipe and bake our cake living the values in the Bible, we will make the truest cake we can.

Like a lot of people, I'm in search of truth, not perfection, so why expect perfection? The recipe I'm sharing with you tells us to expect some imperfections along the way. As such, your business is not going to be perfect either. Therefore, you must communicate with those who are following you. While I am the leader, I am not perfect! I do not expect perfection from myself, so I do not expect perfection from you. As Voltaire said, *"Perfect is the enemy of good."* Do not let your pursuit of perfection stop you from making good improvements. Once you realize this, something great happens—you learn to accept yourself for who you are. The cake tastes much sweeter this way.

Leadership situations may change, and while we adapt to the change around us, we must not let our values change out of convenience. We use the term situational leadership loosely. Situations do not provide us with the latitude to change our values because of a situation. Truth and integrity are the key ingredients for making a great tasting cake for your own life and for your business.

When I was a squadron commander, if you got a DUI (a citation for Driving Under the Influence), that was a serious breach of values. There is no situational leadership there. "Well sir, it was late at night," or, "I was all the way across town in Scottsdale (Arizona) Sir." I didn't care. It was a DUI. The squadron leadership team gave everyone the tools to avoid this, and sometimes, people chose not to use them. Once those values were clearly articulated, we were able to inspire the squadron members to follow that rule willingly.

Through my time in the Air Force, the last squadron I commanded had no DUIs. I am humbled enough to realize this was not because I was the commander, or my leadership style. To a certain degree it was simply luck. At my retirement party we found out the NCOs would tell their troops the rules and say, "Hey don't worry about Colonel Smiley killing you if you get a DUI, we'll kill you first."

Leaders cannot change or create a culture by themselves. They need others to help bake the chocolate cake. At my retirement party, we all shared the no-DUI-chocolate-cake. Then, a month after I retired, there was an airman in my former squadron who received a DUI. Needless to say, my successor was not too happy!

Emotional Strength and Fortitude

Sometimes being a leader can be very lonely. You are the big boss, and sometimes people do not want to give you bad news. Leaders can be intimidating just by nature of being a leader, but the servant leader embodies these special leadership attributes:

- Selflessness
- Compassion
- Humility

- Credibility
- Sacrifice
- Love

As a servant leader, we should routinely make employee engagement and feedback part of our daily routine. Part of our focus should be on removing roadblocks and fixing problems that impact the performance of the business and our employees. As a servant leader, we must make ourselves available to receive feedback and suggestions at all levels. I very seldom make a final decision without consulting key leaders in the company because my perspective as the leader can be different from the perspectives of those in the field or from our staff specialists (e.g., accounting, contracting, human resources, operations, and the legal department), our directors, and vice presidents.

Sometimes people may filter information given to the boss. Let us chalk that one up to human nature. So, the question is, how do you get through the filter? When you need feedback, always go to the root. I found this out during my two tours as a commander in the Air Force. When I spoke to the younger troops, without the Non-Commissioned Officers (NCOs) in the room, that is when I got a unique perspective, or as the young troops called it, "the low down." The separate meetings were not designed to go around the NCOs in their chain of command, they were to reinforce the fact I am responsible for each and every person and their families. I had to find out what was the bad news or issues no one wanted to bring to the commander.

The interesting thing is what some perceived to be bad news was not bad news at all. It was usually something small like, "Sir, we would really like big screen TVs for the dormitory." That's, it? New big screen TVs? My young troops got new big screen TVs for the dormitory. That, my friends, is one small example of servant leadership.

Clear and honest communication is the balance beam on which leadership stands. You gather the people you are leading, and you tell them who you are. This is a mantra I tell my staff regularly:

"I am passionate about Sonoran Technology. I'm committed to you and your families, I do my best to be fair, reasonable and I deal with facts. I have zero tolerance for incivility, harassment, or any kind of discrimination, and I always put people before profit. This is who I am, this is the company you work for, and these are some of my expectations for myself and my expectations for you. Do not be afraid to give me bad news. I am an adult—I can handle it."

Personally, I do not know any organization that does not have periodic communication problems. If you go back to when you were a kid and you messed up and fessed up to your mom or dad, you knew what the consequences were. On the other side of that, there's more to life than negative consequences, there are also positive consequences when you do something good. Leaders, when doling out consequences, must keep that in mind.

I come from a school of thought that believes not everyone has the personality or character traits to lead others. These individuals just don't possess the will or inclination to sacrifice, be humble, or be selfless. Based on my experience as a leader, quite often you must put yourself second, third, fourth, and sometimes fifth in line.

Servant leadership must be about something bigger than you, and some people just aren't built that way.

Success does not determine the quality of a leader. There is a distinct difference between effective leaders and successful leaders. There are leaders who understand it is not about me, it is about us. These are the people who are, oftentimes, effective leaders. Effective leaders focus on making those around them better. The successful leader, meanwhile, can build successful companies or organizations behind him or her, but their focus is usually internal, not external. They care about the people around them second to themselves. These are the leaders that talk about all the great stuff they've accomplished, without recognizing those that helped them.

In the fall of 2022, I was returning to my car with a basket full of items from Costco. I saw a young man collecting what seemed like a hundred shopping carts. The young man looked tired, beat down, and distraught. I said to him, "I just want you to know, without you, Costco wouldn't make a lot of money today." Astonished, he replied, "Thanks sir, I needed to hear that." The lesson here is that people need to feel valued for their work. When you hear one of your employees say, "I'm just a _____ (fill in the blank)," that's a clear sign you need to take your leadership efforts to the next level.

It could be something as simple as leaving your office and meeting with your employees in their space, and sincerely asking, "How are things going? Is there anything you need from me?" Your employees not only need to see, but really *feel* you care about them. Then, you must make sure that your caring is consistent, sincere, and from the heart.

"My leadership and human interaction experiences reinforce these sentiments, and I believe they are the foundation of a thriving and healthy organizational culture."
—Paul Smiley

Effective leaders focus on demonstrating character, trust, integrity, and doing what's best for the team. Conversely, but not always, some leaders pride themselves on being successful and their reputation. If you are a faith-based leader, remember this: *Your reputation is what other people think of you. Your character is what God knows to be true about you.*

You don't need to care about your reputation if your character is in check. Your reputation will be built exactly as you want it if you live in your character and act instead of talking. I heard this old preacher once say, "the life you live will preach your funeral."

Finally, I see leadership as a gift. You have the privilege to lead, and you don't want to screw it up. Because when you mess up as a leader it not only impacts you, but it can also impact a lot of other people.

This is a fact every leader needs to embrace. As leaders, we must make smart decisions because if we don't make smart decisions, it can impact the livelihood of people who work for us. Leadership is not a title. Leadership is action.

The Leadership Light

A very common quote used today to determine if you are a leader or not is, "look behind you. Are there people following you?" This is an old leadership adage that has been around for decades. Nonetheless, congratulations, you are a leader of some sort. Now the real questions are what kind of leader are you? Are people **willingly** following you? That second question is one that oftentimes doesn't get much attention. However, over the years, I have come to appreciate the immeasurable value that willing followers bring to an organization.

Leaders are like lighthouses. They can save others from tragedy, or guide followers to growth and opportunity. The thing is lighthouses only work if their light is on.

Oftentimes we call ourselves leaders, but our leadership light isn't on. A leader that is not putting their skills to use is like a dim lighthouse in a storm. It serves no purpose.

When I leave the house in the morning, I double check to see that my leadership light is on, that I'm being an example, I'm treating others with respect and dignity, I'm being patient, and I'm using words that matter. That is how I can tell that my leadership light is on so I can be the best leader I can be. We have a chocolate cake to bake after all.

Assessing Your Leadership Qualities

There is a common truth we sometimes don't like to hear; we all have blind spots. Why? Because I believe we live in a "see and judge world." I remember going through Mission Crew Commander training on the E-3 AWAC jet in 1994 at Tinker Air Force Base in Oklahoma City. My primary instructor's personal appearance was not what I expected for an Air Force Major. Wrinkled and high-watered flight suit, Air Force issued-black framed glasses, and a really bad haircut. These were all the exterior things I saw and a classic example of prejudging someone.

As it turns out, the gentleman was the best flight instructor I ever had during my entire Air Force career. He was very smart in all facets of the jet, crew leadership, mission operations, and mission execution. His demeanor was poised, confident, calming, and patient. Although we never flew together again, years later, I saw someone who looked like my former flight instructor. That earlier "see and judge" mistake was a stark reminder we need to be aware of our blind spots and focus on seeing everyone through the eyes of God. One day, I hope to run into my former instructor and offer him a heartfelt and sincere apology.

Here's another blind spot example. My daughter Rachel introduced me to a young man she was seeing. He had a man bun, scraggly beard, and a few tattoos. His appearance triggered a bias that I did not know existed in me. The first time he met me he said, "Hey, dude..." Shocked and agitated, I said, "Stop, go outside, come back in, and let's try it again." Afterwards, Rachel told me, "You know Dad, you can be really intimidating!" That blew my mind! Me? Intimidating? That's not me! On the outside, Rachel's comment did not bother me, but on the inside, it triggered an emotion, revealing an internal reality to which I had been blind. Other people do not always see us the way we see ourselves.

That following Monday, I told my Chief Financial Officer, Gina, about the comment Rachel made about me being intimidating. "Gina, can you believe that?" I asked. Without skipping a beat, Gina replied, "Oh yeah, for sure, you can be intimidating at times...but it's not the mean spirited or bullying type of intimidation." Shocked, I asked Gina to tell me more.

She told me, "You can be intimidating, but not in a bad way. It is the way you carry yourself, your demeanor, and it makes people want to not let you down. You are a business owner with lots of responsibilities, hundreds of employees that are counting on you, and that means you must be a serious guy a lot of the time. You do your job, you take care of your family, and the Sonoran Family, and that can be intimidating to some people, but it's not a bad thing."

As leaders, we must set high standards if we want great results. Equally important is the fact we must adhere to the standards ourselves if we expect people to follow them. For example, if office hours start at 8am, we should be there at 8am or before. If people see you come in later, you have unknowingly set the standard. You must be the example you want people to follow.

Leadership Self-Assessment

The BOLT test is a great tool I have used over the years to analyze different types of leaders, personalities, and to better determine who is best suited to lead in different circumstances. The BOLT Leadership Model is a popular approach used to assess, understand, and to improve team dynamics. There is not a specific named creator of the BOLT Leadership Assessment, but rather it has been developed as a tool within the broader organizational and industrial psychology field and has been utilized by various management consultants and trainers.

The model categorizes individuals into four primary archetypes based on their default behavior patterns: *Bull, Owl, Lamb, and Tiger.*

- **Bull**: Dominant and assertive leaders who value getting things done quickly and efficiently. They are direct, decisive, competitive, and pragmatic.

- **Owl**: Detailed and analytical leaders who focus on precision, accuracy, and thoroughness. They are thoughtful, organized, logical, and methodical.
- **Lamb**: Harmonious and amicable leaders who value relationships and people's feelings. They are patient, cooperative, dependable, and supportive.
- **Tiger**: Influential and expressive leaders who are enthusiastic, charismatic, and value creativity and innovation. They are energetic, optimistic, persuasive, and sociable.

The BOLT assessment can help individuals identify their primary and secondary styles, which can be helpful in increasing self-awareness, understanding others better, and improving interpersonal relationships. As I mentioned earlier, there are several leadership styles attributed to one's personality. The *Hersey-Blanchard Model is a* "leadership model that focuses on the ability and willingness of individual employees."[18] This model is also known as the *Situational Leadership Model*, and different from other models, ignores the thought that businesses need one way to approach leadership. Instead, this model can help define an adaptive leadership style. This is important to leaders because they can adapt to each employee's abilities and experiences to grow with them.

Unlike large businesses, where they usually have a large pool of talent to choose from, small businesses typically have limited resources in the early start-up stages. This means the leadership style the small business owner uses for the culture you want to develop is critical because once it is in place, it will be difficult to change. All eyes are on you as the boss.

Example BOLT Leadership Assessment Questions

The following are sample statements that might be included in a BOLT leadership assessment. Read each of the following statements and ask yourself how much you agree with each and then rate your agreement with each statement on a scale (e.g., from 1, "strongly disagree," to 5, "strongly agree").

- **Bull**
  - I enjoy working in a demanding environment.
  - I make decisions quickly and confidently.
  - I am comfortable taking charge in group settings.
  - I am focused on getting results.

- **Owl**
  - I pay careful attention to details.
  - I prefer to think things through before making decisions.
  - I value accuracy and precision.
  - I feel comfortable with routines and structures.

- **Lamb**
  - I place high value on harmony within my team.
  - I am sensitive to the feelings of others.
  - I am often the peacemaker in conflicts.
  - I enjoy supporting others and helping them succeed.

- **Tiger**
  - I enjoy exploring innovative ideas and innovative solutions.
  - I am naturally enthusiastic and expressive.
  - I am comfortable being the center of attention.
  - I like to inspire and motivate others.

Now, total up your scores. The highest category is your primary leadership style, and the next highest is your secondary BOLT leadership style.

By understanding our own leadership temperament and the traits of others, small business owners can better lead, manage, communicate, motivate, and collaborate within their teams.

Let us put the BOLT assessment to the test. Let's say you have an employee who has consistently been one of your top-notch performers. This person is always on time, and often is the first one in the office. Their work is impeccable and suddenly they are struggling. Their work is noticeably not as good, and their once polished appearance is now kind of disheveled. Like all your other employees, you sincerely care about this employee's welfare. Who is the leader in your company who possesses the right temperament for the situation, that you send to help this employee? Well, I can tell you from personal experience, it's not the leader with bull or tiger characteristics. A leader with a primarily lamb temperament traits is likely your best choice.

On the same token, say you must send one of your key staff members to a budget meeting to ensure your department gets the money it needs to meet the company's goals for the upcoming year. Maybe you've attended a meeting early in your career and you know it is a "dog-eat-dog" type of meeting where every department head is fighting for money. Who do you send to that meeting? The lamb or the bull? This is a situation when don't send the lamb, you release the bull!

Even though you are the owner, leader, and boss, it's important to understand you are not required to have to have all the answers or lead every conversation. The goal is to surround yourself with other smart leaders, managers, and subject matter experts.

A smart business owner focuses on knowing what your team's strengths are, what your strengths are, and send the right leader (right fit talent) to accomplish the task at hand.

I think you will find each of us possess some of all four of the BOLT personality traits. The key here is to find out which one is your predominant trait and to develop others to complement you. Your understanding of yours and others' personality traits can also help you deal effectively with others. Here are some ways to deal with the assorted styles that you will find on your team:

How to Interact with a Bull

Bulls prefer directness and getting right to the point. Do not go off on tangents or you will lose them. Be confident in your dealings with them and make sure you know what you are talking about as they can be a bit impatient. Do not try to tell them they are wrong; they need to be shown the facts to make their own determinations. Do not use frills and fluff when dealing with a "bull."

How to Interact with an Owl

Owls are generally introverted and serious in nature. Everything should be analyzed, and all questions should be fully answered for an owl to feel most comfortable. Too much excitement is unsettling to an owl—they like stability and routine or they are out of their comfort zone. You cannot rush an owl to decide, and it is best to present the facts clearly and concisely and let an owl make up its own mind. The owl is very sharp and very dependable. You only get one chance with an owl, so do not mess it up.

How to Interact with a Lamb

Lambs are generally more soft-spoken and move at a much slower pace. They are good listeners, but they do have a tough time making decisions. Patience is a virtue when dealing with a lamb. They can be outgoing or introverted and are generally kind and amenable. Lambs do not feel comfortable with too much force or directness. Use your words and actions wisely and at a slower pace to make them feel the most comfortable. You must gently nudge a lamb. The lamb will flee if frightened.

How to Interact with a Tiger

Tigers are playful, so relevant chit chat is fine before launching into the core of a discussion. Tigers will not give you clues as to what they are thinking and are fast and direct communicators. They are a little more flexible and playful compared to the bull; when pushed, the tiger will hold its own.

When we as leaders understand that there is something special and valuable in the special styles on our team, we realize our teams are stronger. It is up to us as leaders to know how to best lead and inspire each person on our team.

There are Different Levels of Leadership

When we started Sonoran Technology, I considered myself a novice business owner even though I considered myself to be an experienced leader in general terms. In Jim Collins book, *Good to Great*, he talks about levels of leadership, which he lists five different levels of leaders, which I have broken down here[19]:

Level 1 leader: Highly Capable Individual

Thought leader and global speaker Liz Wiseman calls highly capable individuals "impact players." As an individual, they are invaluable. According to Jim Collins, this first level of leadership is about having good individual skills. The qualities of Level 1 leaders include productive contribution through talent, knowledge, skills, and good working habits. They make a meaningful contribution to the team and have a good understanding of the task at hand. They do a good job and apply their knowledge effectively.

Level 2 leader: Contributing Team Member

Team building is a key skill of the Level 2 leader. They use their areas of working genius to benefit the team and achieve group objectives. They know how to **help the team succeed** and they complete jobs effectively, successfully, and productively. They use their knowledge and skills to help others work as a team. Impact players are also found here in Level 2 and can step up to become Level 3s or higher.

Level 3 leader: Competent Manager

This hard-working impact player and team star has **excellent management skills**. They effectively and efficiently pursue organizational goals with their team. Given that most organizations are keen to achieve goals and objectives, a Level 3 leader is an asset.

Level 4 leader: Effective Leader

According to Jim Collins the Level 4 Leader is great at **stimulating higher performance standards** from their people. They're not Level 5, but they are effective leaders who can motivate departments or companies to meet goals and performance objectives. They catalyze commitment to a clear and compelling vision, and help teams achieve the goals that bring it to life.

Level 5 leader: Great Leader

As we said earlier, Jim Collins found that the **skills of levels 1 to 4 were present in Level 5 leaders,** but these great leaders also had an **"extra dimension"**: a paradoxical blend of personal humility (e.g., "I never stopped trying to become qualified for the job").

While I was not new to leadership when starting Sonoran, I was new to running a small start-up business. My Air Force career as an officer prepared me to lead people, yet the business world was different because I did not have that rank or legitimate power afforded in the military. When your rank or title is not uniformly understood, leaders need to evaluate themselves adequately and honestly. When you get commissioned in the military, whether it is as an Air Force Lieutenant or an Army Lieutenant, or you enter the NCO ranks, you are instantly expected to take on a leadership role. Yet, getting commissioned seldom discusses or explains what level of leadership you have achieved.

Too often the big boss would say "Okay, you're a leader, you've got this." No, you don't!

Be careful not to throw young leaders in roles to motivate, inspire, and lead one of the most complicated species on the planet—humans! We are a complex and diverse web of people with backgrounds, languages, values, and opinions.

New leaders need guidance and mentorship. Although you may not know it at the time, what you have is a level one leader and suddenly they are dealing with personalities, problems, events, and decisions designed for a more experienced and higher level of leadership. The newly minted leader suddenly realizes the magnitude and scope of responsibility they have is much greater than they previously imagined.

Today, using Jim Collin's definition, I would consider myself a level five leader. Over three decades of leadership and life experiences (successes, failures, disappointments, grace, mercy, faith), and a long list of supporters and mentors, have helped me get to this point. Yet, there is more work to be done. Level five leadership does not mean you are finished. In order to stay ahead of the competition and continuously inspire people, small business owners, mentors, and leaders must continue to be passionate life-long learners because the world and people are constantly changing.

Finally, my faith has helped me make better decisions. I have faith that I will be provided the tools, resources (my gifts and talents), and if necessary, people to help me effectively lead and accomplish what needs to be done. My moral purpose in starting Sonoran Technology was not to make money, or be successful, it was about creating life change for myself and our employees. With that moral purpose in mind, I make sure my leadership light is on every day, to inspire my team to willingly help us build the chocolate cake of life change. Finally, becoming an effective leader and mentor is a process, a life-long journey. As such, we need to assess and reassess our leadership light by asking for, and openly receiving honest feedback.

CHAPTER 3 TAKEAWAYS

- Leadership requires "willing" followers.

- Real teamwork is inspirational.

- "Perfection is the enemy of good" —Voltaire.

- Leadership can be lonely at times.

- Make sure your leadership light is on

- Are you a Bull, Tiger, Owl, or Lamb?

Taking Care of People

Without people, leaders would have no one to lead. Effective leadership and willing followers are what make all businesses successful, profitable, and sustainable. Now one could argue that technology and artificial intelligence (AI) are taking over jobs that were once performed by humans. Correct, but not all jobs. Not the ones that are emotionally interactive, the jobs and professions that require face-to-face interaction and cooperation.

Today, for the most part, certain types of sales interactions are technology driven. Kiosks have been a part of the sales paradigm for years. We see them in grocery stores, retail stores, banks, even at the airport. No doubt the biggest consumer change during the past 20 years is online retail, which I believe is still in its infancy. This brings us to the question: Which jobs and professions still require business owners to hire and retain what the Disney Institute refers to as the "right fit talent?"

According to the Disney Institute: *"When hiring, we consider a candidate's attitude, not just skills alone, which aids in matching the right person to the right role. We believe that attitude outweighs aptitude … think about how important the selection process can be for creating your desired workplace culture."*[20]

When Sonoran Technology partnered with the Disney Institute on a Leadership Development and Customer Services contract with the Department of Veterans Services, I was amazed at the effectiveness of the "right fit talent" approach. During our team visit to Disney World in Orlando, Florida, our interaction with cast members, hospitality teams and other support personnel validated that to have a high performing company culture, willing followers, and overall success, it starts with the hiring process which takes the candidates attitude into consideration.

There are professional personal services such as doctors' offices, dentists, hair salons, barbershops, restaurants, and many others where delivering exceptional service is the primary job. One way business owners can achieve and maintain exceptional customer service standards is to hire and retain the best talent possible. Here we are today decades later, and one of the most pressing issues is workforce development. What is workforce development? Chances are it means different things to different people in different industries. For the small business owner however, workforce development has always been around but we seldom, if ever, used the term.

When we started Sonoran Technology, our focus was on hiring the "right fit talent" and then conducting training and development programs to significantly improve organizational and individual performance.

Today, I believe there are three recent events that have brought workforce development challenges to the forefront. First, the COVID-19 pandemic which had a major economic impact on the world economy and job loss. Second, technology. During the pandemic, suppliers and consumers had to find new and innovative ways to deliver and purchase goods and services. Third, generational changeover, meaning the baby boomers (those born between the years 1946 and 1964), coming to the end of their careers and being replaced with a younger workforce or technology. In a 2023 paper by Johns Hopkins University, the workforce was broken down by generation to show the following percentages[21]:

• Baby Boomers (1946-64) – 18.6%	Gen X (1965-80) – 34.8
• Millennials (1981-96) – 38.6%	Gen Z (1997-2012) – 11.6%

The simple truth is hiring, training, and retaining the best talent has become more complicated and difficult. Every business is searching for and fighting for the exceptional group of people who want to work for you; for something more than a paycheck. Unfortunately, too many business owners have settled on, forced or not, hiring the wrong fit talent. Hiring just anyone is not a long-term solution to the workforce development problem.

Does anyone have the right answer? To be totally honest with you, I don't know. What I do know is that the process to finding solutions to the workforce development challenge lies in defining the problem before suggesting solutions, like Albert Einstein suggests:

> *"If I had only one hour to save the world, I would spend fifty-five minutes defining the problem, and only five minutes finding the solution."*

> — *Albert Einstein*

When we first define what hiring talented, smart, and committed employees looks like, we can begin resolving the workforce development challenge. In 2012, five years after going into business, I had a revelation about what services Sonoran performed. It was obvious, our market was aircrew training, courseware development, and air operations support. We provided a host of military operations support services including, but not limited to, IT help desk, logistics services and so on. However, the bigger picture was that we are in the "people business." When I looked at it from that view point, it really changed my perspective.

Anytime the company had a vacancy, we asked the program manager, "Why?"

Like Albert Einstein, our focus was to first define the problem. Why did the person leave the company? Family, location, pay and benefits, or our culture?

Once we answered those questions through mandatory exit interviews, our managers and recruiters produced solutions which increased our employee retention rate to a record high of 95%. Prior to that, we simply didn't know what we did not know. Site visits with our employees across the country provided great insights into how they felt about the company, both good, and what needed to change. To take care of your customers, you must have employees who are cared for, who trust the leadership, and who embrace and support the company's culture. This is the foundation for employees who willingly follow you and become what we call "employees for life." At some point in time, employees will eventually leave your company, but the relationships, if you inspired them, will last a lifetime.

I have a friend who owns an impressive Mexican restaurant in Arizona. One day, I went to his restaurant for lunch and the food, woefully, did not meet my expectations as it had for the past ten years.

When a server came by, I said, "Excuse me, the food is cold in the middle." She apologized and offered to warm it up in the microwave, but I said no thanks. Later, when she returned with the check, the main meal was on there even though I only had chips, salsa, and a soft drink. I pointed this out and she replied, "I'm sorry I can't take it off the check." I thought about it, and I was kind of ticked off on the drive home because I knew my friend who owns the restaurant would be extremely disappointed with my customer experience. A few weeks later, I was driving by and figured I would stop in to see if the owner was there. He was. I said, "Pete, I came here a couple weeks ago, and I had a cold chimichanga and the server told me she couldn't take it off the bill." He was upset, apologized, and asked if I would stay for dinner. Now, I did not go in looking for free food or drink, I just went in to share my customer experience with him as a fellow business owner. If this was my restaurant I would've like to know if something like this happened.

This event is not necessarily a result of not hiring the right fit talent, it could be a lapse in customer service training. Every business owner at some point and time will have an opportunity to take immediate corrective actions to protect their brand or reputation. Had that been the first time I had been at the restaurant; I probably would not have gone back. I am 100% sure my friend Pete saw this as a "teachable" opportunity for that employee—as an opportunity to correct and encourage. As I mentioned earlier, no one is perfect and the worst outcome in this scenario is for that employee to believe that mistakes are not tolerated. Good for my friend Pete; that server still works there.

Another notable example of how to establish trust with your people working the front line was an experience I had with the Disney Institute in Florida with the Department of Veteran Affairs (VA). I was invited down to Orlando to observe how they operate behind the scenes. When I checked into the hotel, the concierge said, "Hello, Mr. Smiley, welcome to Disney. We knew you were coming. Anything I can do to make your day better?"

I said, "Well, I've actually got the taste for some chocolate milk and cookies." Why I wanted milk and cookies is still a mystery, but I did. I went on my tour of the park, the hotels, and several restaurants in the park. I was literally gone for the whole day, and when I returned to my room, there was a quart of chocolate milk in a glass container with some homemade peanut butter cookies, my favorite. To say the least, I was stunned. That Disney employee created such an unexpected event for me, I had almost forgotten I even made the remark when I checked in. Yet, she not only remembered, but she also saw to it that it was delivered to my room before I returned. That was roughly ten years before the time of this writing, and it made such an impression on me that here I am telling the story again. The Disney adage of "under-promise and overdeliver" did not even apply because there was no promise, just something delivered unexpectedly. Working with Disney was like a master's degree in taking care of people.

Food for thought as it relates to hiring the right fit talent in the uncertain future is to dismiss the growing opinion that the personal and professional attributes that businesses are looking for in a newly hired employee are not as important in the new remote work environment. Do not believe that for one minute! Why wouldn't qualifications, experience, character, honesty, integrity, timeliness, professionalism, and civility be important in a remote work environment? I am from the opposite school of thought. Working remotely requires a new level of discipline and personal accountability. Remember, regardless of what kind of business you are in, every business owner operates in the people business.

Embracing the "We are in the People Business" Concept

On a beautiful fall day in November 2009, I made the mistake of going to the local Home Depot on a Saturday. I was looking to buy a BBQ grill, and I asked the salesperson if I could buy a grill that was already assembled.

"Sorry Sir, we don't sell them assembled," he said, casually.

That is when it hit me.

This is a community where the median age is 73 years old. What if the store's local customers have some form of arthritis or vision problems? I thought to myself, "There is no way they are buying a grill that is not already assembled." In fact, *I* didn't want to assemble a grill.

Market research is one of my favorite pastime activities, especially when it comes to consumer buying trends and habits. I spoke with the store manager and told him I was an Adjunct Professor at Arizona State University West campus and wanted to conduct a little market research. After sharing my thoughts on selling pre-assembled grills based on the local demographics, I said to him, "Why don't you try selling preassembled grills? I will come back in three to four months and see how it worked out."

The next time we met the manager said, "You wouldn't believe how many pre-assembled grills we sold!"

It is impossible to know exactly why the store's pre-assembled grill sales increased so dramatically during that time, but the store's efforts to better service their aging customer base probably had a lot to do with it. This calls back to that old business saying that if you don't take care of your customers, someone else will.

Oftentimes, competition is not about price, it's about the

service and the buying experience. A customer that has had a positive and rewarding experience is the first step in achieving a "customer for life" following.

Here's another example. I have been a USAA Insurance customer for close to 42 years. I get calls from GEICO, State Farm, and other insurance companies, all offering to beat the USAA price. Maybe they can, maybe they can't. Like a lot of USAA customers, I ask these other insurance companies, "Can you beat USAA's customer service?"

Why would I change from a company that has always delivered for me? To save $100 a year? Most people will gladly pay a little more in exchange for world-class customer service! Do not get me wrong, I'm not saying USAA is a perfect company, no company is. But when you find a company you can trust, one that provides exceptional customer service, coupled with a fair price, this equates to value. That's the interesting thing about value, it means different things to different consumers.

Consider an HVAC (heating, ventilation, and air-conditioning) technician working in Arizona during the summer months. It is August, and it is 118 degrees outside. When the air conditioning goes out, homeowners are looking for a reliable and professional HVAC company to fix their air conditioning problem as soon as possible. For most of the Arizona population, air conditioning is not just a nice thing to have, it is a must have.

One of my former employees, who was a senior citizen at the time, had her air conditioning unit break during one of the hottest days in August. When she called a local HVAC company, they told her it would take at least three days to get somebody out to repair the unit. It seemed like their only option was to go stay with family or get a hotel room.

For anyone, not to mention two senior citizens, to live in such heat is inherently dangerous. This example reinforces my earlier point that servant leaders understand that regardless of the name of their business, we are always in the people business. We knew exactly what actions Sonoran needed to take in this scenario; help get our employee and their family to air-conditioned lodging immediately. Our company took action, and this initiative by our corporate staff members clearly illustrates our company culture of taking care of our employees. Delegating certain decision-making authority to my supervisors and managers also expedited the process attending to the needs of our employees.

You want to know why an employee says, "This is the best company I have ever worked for!"? Look for ways to say, "Yes" first, rather than starting with "No!"

A leader's character is often defined by how we treat other people. My older sister says she can tell a lot about a guy if his shoes are clean or dirty. I tell my daughter, "You can tell a lot about your date by the way he treats the server. Chances are the way he treats them is how he will treat you ..."

Our personal lives are not much different from business lives in the sense that we are more effective, and life is more rewarding, when we are surrounded by the right fit talent. We are simply better human beings when we are around selfless, loving, kind, respectful, trustworthy, and civil-minded people.

My professional experience in the Air Force and as a small business owner has taught me you cannot have people with an "it's all about me" attitude on the team. Sooner or later that person will become a distraction and can threaten the culture of the organization.

While the personality attributes and skills a person brings to the organization, whether in work or in their personal life, are important, I'm convinced none are more important than attitude. I've heard people say, "you cannot train attitude." The question, rather, is do you want to spend valuable time trying to change someone's attitude? The attitude we look for as business owners during the interview or hiring process should reflect the culture of our business. Going back to Disney's "right fit talent" model, if you asked a Disney employee "What does Disney do?" they would tell you "Our number one job is to make people happy." So, who does Disney hire? They hire happy people.

For example, let's say you are in the final interview with a candidate whose resume is a spot-on match in terms of experience, skill level, and education requirements listed in the job description. On paper, they appear to be the right fit for the job and your company. The problem is, you can't really tell from an application what their attitude is like, even during an interview. Something I've learned with hiring the right fit talent is that a resume says what we do or what we have done. It does not reflect who we are on the inside.

Normally, it can take a few weeks or even months before you are convinced your HR department hit a recruiting home run. Will the new hire adapt, embrace, and defend your company's culture? Their work ethic, behaviors and "we, not me" attitude will shine through and hopefully be contagious. Just the opposite is true when we hire a person who is not the right fit. The substantial difference here is, it takes a little more time for the employee to reveal themselves. Chances are, during the interview process it was all an act, because they needed a job or for some other reason. This is not to say the candidate is not qualified, doesn't have the required experience, or that they are a bad person. For whatever reason(s), they simply cannot adapt to the company's culture, can't work in a team environment, or don't have high regard for the company's policy on civility.

In the defense contracting business, most of the labor category salaries and benefits are pre-determined when we submit our price proposal to the federal government. During the job interview process, shortly after the contract is awarded, there is a point where we discuss, in great detail, employee pay and benefits. Rarely is there a situation where our hiring or program manager and the new hire cannot mutually agree on the terms of employment, pay and benefits, etc. At Sonoran, it is standard operating procedure to put everything we are offering an employee, and what we expect from them in writing. The final agreement is signed by the company president, and only the company president. In my view, the employment offer letter says to the new employee, "Our President stands by the contents in the offer letter." It's the first promise we make in our relationship with our employees. This is where trust begins and where trust begins to nourish.

The interview process, whether in person or virtual, is a great time to get to know the person seeking employment. It is an opportune time to find out what the person does for fun, what their favorite holiday is, or what they are passionate about. My favorite question is: "How do you like to be rewarded?" I found this to be an extremely valuable question that comes in handy when a reward opportunity presents itself. For example, we have employees who would rather have a few extra PTO (personal time off) days rather than a bonus check. Why? Because they value time off more than a $200 gift card. Bottom line, people have different reward values and when you connect the two, people tend to feel valued.

During my time as an adjunct instructor at Arizona State University's West Valley Campus, I would ask both graduate and undergraduate seniors, "Tell me about yourself."

These amazing cohorts of future leaders and business professionals would all say the same thing as they went around the room. "My name is X, my major is Y, blah, blah, blah." Once they finished, and I stopped making all sorts of unprofessional faces, I said, "Great. Now, do it again, but this time, tell me about you."

It literally took three times before they got the clue.

"Oh, okay. I am married. I have two kids. I grew up in Michigan. I am a big college football fan. I do not like crowds. I'm super happy on cloudy days..."

You get the point. This was a drill to help my students prepare for the best job interview they would ever have. This simple classroom exercise set the tone for the business leadership course they signed up for. My goal was to prepare them to wear the "I'm the right fit talent you've been looking for" banner in every aspect of their professional life. In this new workforce development challenged world we live in, visionary leaders have started developing and training the workforce they want and need.

We can find the case and point at United Airlines. In December 2021, United Airlines and its subsidiary, United Aviate Academy leased a state-of-the-art training facility at Phoenix Goodyear Airport. The goal was to help reduce the on-going pilot shortage. United invested in its flight academy with the goal of training 5,000 new pilots by the end of 2030, including at least 50% who are women and/or people of color.

On January 25, 2023, United Airlines graduated 51 new pilots from United Aviate Academy, and close to 80% of the graduates were women and people of color, fulfilling a key diversity marker they set.[22] United Airlines executives took on the workforce challenge by developing not only the workforce they needed, but the workforce they wanted. Too often, when budgets are strapped and revenue is low, training is the first thing to hit the budget chopping block. The leadership at United Airlines made one of the best investments a business can make, they invested in their people. Launching United's Aviate Academy at the Phoenix Goodyear Airport was a visionary leadership move that could give United Airlines a leg up on the competition.

Employee Retention is Serious Business

Early in the start-up of the business, our contracts manager was a former Air Force contracting officer. She was efficient, smart and had a wealth of knowledge about federal contracting. As I mentioned earlier, it is important not only to know your employee skills and talents, strengths, and weaknesses, but also what makes them happy. In this case, our contracts manager's happiness was found in shoes, which she affectionately called "her babies."

One day, she asked Pete and I to help her move to a new home she had recently purchased. When we moved the contents of her closet, there were over 75 pairs of women shoes in their individual boxes, with a picture of the shoes on the front of the box. At first, I jokingly thought to myself, "Wow, she really needs some professional counseling." Then it hit me, her mindfulness and organizational skills, which were demonstrated at work, were also part of her personal life as well, and what made her happy was shoes!

What does this have to do with employee retention? I once heard someone say, "The way people feel about you, is the way you make them feel." This quote is fool proof!

For example: "You know Bob? Yes, the guy over in the shipping department; he is one hell of a guy. Kind, genuinely respectful, and always has something positive to say. Bob is literally the kind of guy who would give you his last dollar if you needed it." You are not going to find many people, if any, who do not like Bob.

Learning from this example, I wanted to make our contracts manager felt special, and the best way to do that is to know what made her happy.

For Christmas, I enjoyed buying gifts for the corporate office staff. Not just any old gift, but something that showed we cared. Of course, I could have given everyone a nice gift card or a gift of some sort. But, if you want to show someone you care about, appreciate, and value them, and what they mean to the company, then go the extra step.

At our corporate company Christmas Party, we each had a personalized Christmas stocking. My contract manager's stocking was in the shape of a high-heeled shoe. Inside, everything, and I mean everything, was shoe related. A piggy bank, tape dispenser for her desk, a martini glass, an oven mitt, and of course a nice gift card to her favorite shoe store. It was not about the gifts that brought her happiness and joy that day, it was the simple fact that we went out his way to show her how much we cared and valued her. It was special, sincere, honest and from the heart.

Another key element of employee retention is **gratitude**. A sincere thank you for staying late or coming in early by the boss may not mean a lot to one person, but to another employee it is priceless. Not everyone is motivated by tangible gifts or public acknowledgement. That is why it is important to spend time getting to know your employees' love language (i.e., what makes them feel appreciated). What inspires, motivates, and rewards them in a way that has meaning? Do this consistently and watch your company's retention rate improve over time.

Right fit talent and employee retention go together. The Disney Institute outlined and coined the idea of the "right fit" talent, and what it means. When you hire the "right fit" talent, you find somebody who believes in your company. You find somebody that believes in your culture. The employees agree to be a part of your culture, and in return they are going to give the company the best they have.[23]

If you're lucky, the new hire that is not right fit talent will reveal themselves during the first 30 days on the job or sooner. Sonoran Technology has had roughly three or four bad hires that made us go, "That was a big mistake." Yet that feeling you have of hiring the wrong fit pales in comparison to the formidable feeling you get from hiring the right fit. Those who are doing interviews for the right fit talent, particularly at the senior leadership level, should feel the weight of the responsibility. "I am at the pointy end of the spear of making sure this is the right fit talent," and they must defend the team and the culture that way.

Employee Engagement Leads to Employee Growth

Businesses who continuously engage with their employees are on the right track towards employee growth and retention. There is a major hotel and casino who at one time had a difficult time maintaining a motivated and experienced housekeeping staff. Customer check-in, which usually happened around 3:00pm, was delayed until hours later. After an "all-hands" meeting with the housekeeping supervisors and the staff, management was told "the reasons it takes so long to clean the rooms was because the housekeeping carts were cumbersome and too heavy to push."

To make matters worse, the hotel floors had a thick carpet, and the housekeepers were typically smaller in stature. The company's leadership team listened and designed a super lightweight cart, and sure enough, housekeepers were much more efficient. The results were instantaneous. It took less time to clean each room, room cleanliness improved because the housekeepers did not feel rushed, and finally, hotel guests were able to check-in at the predesignated time. The new light-weight service cart had numerous benefits. The employees were elated that management listened to their concerns, asked for input, and made changes to their quality of life and work. Morale skyrocketed and the number of employees calling off work decreased significantly. Additionally, customer requests for late check-outs were easier to get, and there were fewer complaints about delayed check-in times.

At Sonoran, our human resources senior manager decided it was time to retire and move on to the next chapter in their life. Our human resources assistant was a great employee. They were happy, motivated, smart, had a positive attitude, and was great at dealing with people's issues. This individual was a natural. The question at the time was do we hire a new and more experienced HR manager, or do we promote our HR assistant to the position?

Being in the people business means taking chances, measuring risk, and listening to what your heart and soul are telling you.

I told our HR assistant we wanted them to consider taking on the senior HR manager's job, and if they wanted it, it was theirs. Our soon to be HR manager sheepishly said, "I don't think I can fill those shoes," meaning they couldn't maintain the level of influence, admiration, and strong relationships the current manager had created with over 250 employees.

Our CFO Gina, who the new manager would report to, said, "We're not looking for a replacement, we're looking for someone to take the senior HR manager's job to a new level." This blunt and straightforward conversation gave the assistant human resources manager the confidence they needed to take the job. The new senior HR manager later told us they were hesitant about taking the job because they thought they would fail, or not live up to our expectations. I shared with the new manager another famous Albert Einstein quote: *"Anyone who has never made a mistake has never tried anything new."*

After hiring the right fit talent, it's important help them grow. This starts with a Personalized Development Plan, more commonly called a PDP. This can be in the form of a formal appraisal or regularly scheduled feedback sessions. When it comes to appraisals, two words come to mind: ***"No surprises."*** An employee should not be surprised by a negative appraisal because leaders have an obligation to give them a chance to correct actions before the final report is done. Excluding regular feedback is a disservice to your employees and your business. Most people assume they are doing a decent job; no news is good news. Experience tells us this is not necessarily true.

For example, if you are feeling fine health wise and never go in for a regular checkup with your doctor, does "no news is good news" still apply? Regular feedback, both positive and corrective actions that need to be taken, is an employee engagement strategy that grows and nurtures what makes your business flourish, **people**.

The Velvet Hammer

As it relates to employee feedback, I lead by the proverbial motto, "Praise in public, correct in private; always." It is foolish to dismiss, disrespect, or even worse, marginalize another person's feelings. Moreover, talking about employee feelings is a very touchy and sensitive topic these days. Regardless, when corrective action is required, feelings should not outweigh the task at hand-effective and timely professional feedback.

When it comes to employee discipline (e.g., non-adherence to company policy, regulations, culture, and accountability), imaginatively, there are two different types of hammers. There is the sledgehammer, which could mean your future employment is on the line and there is the velvet hammer, which is a bit gentler. The velvet hammer implies most behavior or policy infractions can probably be fixed. Determining which hammer to use says a lot about what kind of leader you are. Not good versus bad, but rather your style of leadership. If necessary, either version of the hammer you're using is always done in private. If my leadership team and I are leading effectively, our history has shown the sledgehammer is seldom used.

I had to use a velvet hammer recently; one of our more experienced managers made a pretty grave mistake. Plainly speaking, they were blatantly disrespectful to a customer on numerous occasions and tried to hide it. We understand and appreciate there are usually two sides to the story, but the manager failed to acknowledge the incident when given the opportunity to do so. This begs the question, when does the president, vice president, or someone at the senior leadership level step in? Is this an issue where the senior manager or vice president takes charge, or is it "Hammer Time?" It all depends on your leadership style, company, policy, procedures, or possibly your gut-feeling.

You could be asking yourself, "What course of action did you take?" Good question. First, I traveled to the site to meet with the manager face-to-face. The face-to-face meeting opposed to a virtual meeting let my manager knew that the company was taking this situation seriously. Next, in a private room, I gave the manager an opportunity to tell their side of the story without any interruptions or body language indications of what I was thinking. Third, I referenced the section in our employee handbook that talks about professional behavior, including the last page of the handbook that had the manager's signature.

It was important to remind the manager that they had agreed to follow the company's performance and professional guidelines. Finally, I asked the manager if their behavior violated the company policy that they had agreed to follow.

The goal was not to embarrass the manager, rather to make the point. I specifically asked the manager, "As a leader, how do you expect your team to follow the rules if you don't set the example?" It has been said that "timing is everything" in just about everything we do, and timely corrective action is no exception. However, the issue of timing has become a lot more complicated in the "tele-work" environment. Caution: do not let telework be an excuse for not taking documented corrective actions or recognition and praise for your high performing employees.

When it comes to self-criticism, as leaders, we must also be wary of which hammer we are using on ourselves. I am usually hard on myself initially, that is, until the rational thought process kicks in.

We can ask ourselves "was it an emotional mistake where I just was not thinking? Was it an error of judgment? Did I have the incorrect information, etc.?" Regardless, remember time and history do not go in reverse. You simply cannot undo what has been done. The most important thing is that you are truthful with yourself. As I alluded to earlier, the goal of perfection is a waste of time and energy, both of which are in limited supply for most small business owners. Because I am not a psychiatrist or psychologist, I am uniquely unqualified to suggest to you how to deal with disappointment or failure.

What I can tell you is if you never pick yourself up, you will always be down. At some point as a business owner, leader, and mentor, we will somehow earn a Ph.D. in *"Well, that didn't work out like I thought it would."*

CHAPTER 4 TAKEAWAYS

- During the interview and hiring process consider the candidate's attitude, not just their skills and qualifications.

- Effective leaders understand that regardless of what type of business you own, you're in the **people business.**

- Continuously look for ways to recognize and reward the top performers.

- In order to take care of your employees, you need to know your employees.

- Timely and balanced corrective actions are key to maintaining a positive respected organizational culture.

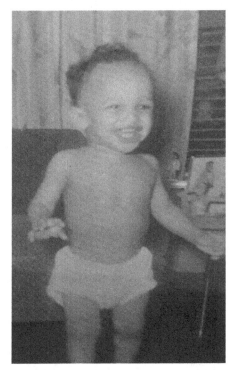

Paul, 1959 at 7 months old

Lt. Colonel Paul A. Smiley, official military photo 2000

Paul, Mr. Mark Cuban, and Ms. Maria Contreras
Sweet, U.S. SBA Administrator, 2016

Paul and U.S. Senator John McCain, 2016

Paul, Malinda, and Rachel Smiley, 2021 Arizona
Veteran Hall of Fame Society Induction Ceremony

Boeing E-3 Airborne Warning and Control
System (AWACS) aircraft

Infrastructure, Policies and Procedures

Small business infrastructure is what the military could call "mission-essential" requirements. Using your company's hiring process for example, is your company using an Equal Employment Opportunity Council (EEOC) approved questions during the interview process that ensures non-discriminatory and only job-related questions are not asked? The same goes for the contents of your company's Employment Offer Letter. Take your most recent hire, for example. Someone in your HR department should have made sure the job title, job description, work hours, pay, benefits, reporting official's name, etc., were correct. Did the newly hired employee read and sign the last page of the Employee Handbook, and is the signature on file? Here's a sample scenario. During the interview process, one of your managers tells the candidate, "The job pays $150,000 annually." However, the position actually pays $125,000 annually. In this scenario you could have a major problem, and probably a legal one as well. These seemingly simple HR employee interview processes are essential elements of business infrastructure, policies, and procedures.

Policies and Procedure Infrastructure

Until recently, some of the small businesses I mentored with never had regularly scheduled staff meetings or team meetings, or what we at Sonoran Technology call "leadership tag-ups." Why? Probably because no one ever told them, or maybe it was because they assumed everyone knew what was going on in the company. The fact is, sending texts or emails does not ensure everyone reads them, or fully understands what the boss is trying to communicate to them. Whether you are a small business with 5 or 125 employees, regularly scheduled leadership meetings, in-person or virtual, are a policy that will improve communications at all levels of your business.

Several years ago, when Sonoran was growing and our geographical footprint was expanding, I instituted a new communications forum called the "leadership tag-up." The purpose of this meeting was to focus on events and issues that could not wait until the next staff meeting. There is an old saying that "little potatoes turn into big potatoes." Problems do not get better; they usually get worse. The "leadership tag-ups" also improved communications company-wide. Having business operations and people living and working in four time zones is beyond challenging, it is downright hard. It seems that when communications are timely and effective, your life and your business become more manageable and less stressful.

At Sonoran, we have monthly corporate staff meetings where the entire staff, and our program managers in the field are required to attend. These virtual meetings were critical during COVID-19 when we worked remotely. The primary purpose of the staff meeting is to ensure everyone understands what is going on company-wide, our top priorities, and what we call "hot topic" items are clearly communicated. From an infrastructure viewpoint, I highly recommend all businesses have a reliable and interactive virtual meeting tool that your staff can access 24/7. I would be remiss if I did not mention the importance of compatible computer hardware and software, which is also part of a business's infrastructure, policy, and procedures. Early on, if someone needed a company laptop or desktop computer, we would purchase it using the company credit card and bam, you were done. We never took into consideration hardware, software, malware, virtual private networks, security, or compatibility requirements. That is, not until a massive 99% completed technical proposal file was corrupted, and we had to rewrite the proposal from scratch. We don't know whether the problem was a result of one employee using an Apple Mac and another employee using a Dell computer, or whether it was due to a computer virus. But we learned a valuable lesson the hard way. Soon after, our new Information Technology (IT) Director instituted a new set of IT policies, procedures, and protocols that not only fixed the problem but mitigated future IT risk. Today, all our company computers have the same software, operating system, security monitoring technology, and are CMMC (Cybersecurity Maturity Model Certification) approved. Every company computer or IT purchase goes through the IT Director, no exceptions.

You might think this is overkill but let me reassure you it is not. When your local church, bank, or mom and pop business is a victim of ransomware, it could be too late for your business to respond. The second-best investment you can make, with people being the first, is to invest in your business infrastructure as soon as you can.

As a Department of Defense (DoD) federal contractor, we were later required to implement and become CMMC compliant. CMMC is a unifying standard and new certification model to ensure that DoD contractors properly protect sensitive information. Here is the kicker—the contractor, whether a small, medium, or large company, must pay for the certification process, and it's not cheap. The good news is the new CMMC requirements not only improved how we protect sensitive Sonoran and government information, but it also gave us an advantage over the competition who were not CMMC certified.

The Bible encourages seeking wise counsel in several passages. One such verse is Proverbs 11:14 which says, "Where there is no guidance, a people fall, but in an abundance of counselors there is safety."[24]

Another relevant verse is Proverbs 12:15, which states, "The way of a fool is right in his own eyes, but a wise man listens to advice."[25]

I have tried to live my personal and professional lives using these verses. Whether you are a person of faith or not, surrounding yourself with, and using, wise counsel is always the right thing to do. At Sonoran, I rely on the senior vice president, vice president, chief financial officer, IT director, contracting director, security manager and the HR manager to provide subject matter expertise. Their departments provide the infrastructure required to effectively execute our business plan. As individuals, they are smart and experienced leaders who I rely on for ideas and suggestions that help me make critical and timely decisions.

The business owner who thinks they can do it all is going to have a tough time leading, not to mention running a growing and profitable business. Chances are the business owner, and their team, will be consumed by stress, and they will isolate people in their company who want to help. The result of trying to carry such a large load will be poor communications and a litany of mistakes and poor decisions.

History has proven the number of tasks a leader can effectively manage varies depending on factors such as their experience, time constraints, delegation skills, and team size.

However, on average, it is widely accepted that a leader or manager can effectively manage 5 to 7 direct reports or projects at a given time. This allows for sufficient attention and support to be given to each individual or project, ensuring its success. It is important for leaders to prioritize and manage their workload effectively, delegating tasks where necessary, and regularly re-evaluating their priorities to ensure they can maintain their focus on what's important.

The span of control really comes into play here, and leaders simply cannot do it all. What happens if the leader gets appendicitis, a kidney stone, or the owner must deal with a family emergency? What happens to the business then? Most new start-up small businesses are one person deep (that would be you), and that person (you) are responsible for a lot of important jobs such as payroll, business development, human resources, and more... you get the point.

Part of having a solid and steady infrastructure means having a contingency plan in place so your business can still operate if you or one of your key staff members can't do their job.

Remember, just like life, being a small business owner is a team sport; you cannot do it alone if you want to grow and succeed.

A critical part of being an effective and wise leader is being able to see through the trees so to speak. Wisdom can help you anticipate what is coming. I'll give you an example. My wife and I were traveling a couple of years ago from Phoenix back to Chicago via a quick stop in Minneapolis. When we arrived, the ticketing agent told us the flight was delayed two hours; it was 10:00PM. I told my wife "We need to go to the nearest hotel. This flight is probably going to be cancelled." Being a well-traveled flier and having a good understanding of the rules and regulations for commercial air operations, it was obvious that one of the pilots scheduled for the Chicago leg of our trip would be out-of-duty hours. Further, the airline did not have a flight attendant crew available.

Even if there are two rested pilots, commercial flights are not allowed to fly without the right complement of flight attendants. Moreover, knowing that the airline was required to provide passenger lodging accommodations for the night, we made our way to one of the two nearby airline-approved hotels ahead of the flight cancellation announcement. It was a chance, based on experience and wisdom, I was willing to take. Why? Because there were approximately 150 passengers on our flight, plus, an unknown, but large number of other passengers in the same predicament from other delays. With a limited number of hotel rooms available, I simply did not want to sleep in the airport lobby the night before a big business meeting in Chicago the next morning.

Bottom line, the wise leader carefully assesses the situation and listens to what is and what is not being said. If possible, seek wise counsel or ask a couple of well thought out questions. Reach back into the experience archives, check the "gut" (whatever that is), make a decision, and live with it. This is one small example of how you transition experience into wisdom. Remember, you do not have to be the smartest person in your company.

While you don't have to be the smartest person in your business, you do need to be credible, trusted, respected, wise, and be the most informed person. Like an orchestra director, you do not have to play all of the instruments to know when something doesn't sound right. You clearly and easily recognize when it should have been a flat versus a sharp note. And with a simple twitch of the leadership baton, you know how and what it takes to fix the problem before it happens again.

Banking Relationships and Your Personality Credit Score

During the past 18 years, I have had the good fortune to sit down and talk with several small and mid-size bank presidents. During those times, I have come away with the same thought: **When it comes to the small business community, access to capital is still a huge problem.** Regardless of what kind of economy the U.S. is operating under; strong, weak, recession, economic downturn, whatever you want to call it, access to capital always seems to be in play. Is the lack of capital the only small business roadblock to growth? Probably not, but it is normally in the top five reasons why small businesses fail. As we witnessed during the COVID-19 pandemic, a lack of operating capital was a key factor in businesses permanently closing their doors. As a small business owner, once you slay the access to capital beast, your company will probably have an opportunity to grow. A good rule of thumb when it comes to financial stability is having access to capital before you need it. Just like with lawyers, don't get a lawyer **when** you need one, have one **before** you need one.

My first small business loan was for $50,000 courtesy of West Valley National Bank with President Candace who taught me the Five Cs of banking we discussed previously. It was 2009, and Sonoran desperately needed the operating capital because we were about to be awarded our first multi-million-dollar defense contract.

One of the five Cs of banking is Character. There is a substantial difference between having a banking account and a banking relationship. Candace was my first real banking relationship.

I knew Candace from our time working with the City of Goodyear Arizona Economic Development Office. We had done a few local speaking engagements together. When I went to Candace's bank to tell her I needed a small line of credit, she said, "Normally I would never do this because you're a brand-new start-up company. But, because I know you and I know your character, your reputation, and your standing in the community, I'm going to do this for you."

One of the first things Candace taught me was about credit scores. From a banking perspective, your credit score is the real you. Although the business was new, I had little debt, and my credit score was above average. However, most of our family's personal assets (home equity, 401K savings, and IRA account) were not liquid assets and did not give me the borrowing power the banks were looking for at the time. Remember, this was during the Great Recession (2007 to 2009) and banks were scared. However, my character and my standing in the community created what I call a personality credit score. A personality credit score, much like a financial credit score, is a measurement of trust. As said before, the foundation of a good relationship is trust. By developing the trust factor of being open, honest, and forthright with Candace, I was able to obtain my first small business line of credit. For that, I thank Candace for taking a chance on me.

In a four-year span, Sonoran went from 75 employees to over 325 employees. Obviously, as a back-up plan, we needed to increase our line of credit strictly for payroll purposes. This is where your business history, credit score, and collateral really come into play. The emphasis here is what I call the "Big C," collateral. Sonoran's line of credit increased from a $150,000 line of credit with a local community bank to a two million dollar line of credit with my friends at Bell Bank. Our Bell Bank advocates not only believed in me, but they also believed in Sonoran Technology as a well-established and highly respected small business with strong financial and zero debt. Today, our banking relationship with Bell Bank solidly built on Sonoran's steadfast performance as a small business, timely and consistent communications, personal and professional relationship with Bell's leadership team, low risks, and unwavering TRUST.

Evaluating Yourself and Your Business

Most small businesses have a threat or two (or three) lurking somewhere within their company. Over the past 17 years, we have found it is important to evaluate your business and yourself regularly.

A SWOT analysis (strength, weakness, opportunity, and threat) is a strategic planning tool that helps individuals and organizations identify their strengths, weaknesses, opportunities, and threats. It was created in the 1960s by Robert Franklin Stewart, a management consultant.[26]

Since starting Sonoran Technology in 2007, each year during our strategic planning session we conduct a SWOT analysis. My team and I are deliberate in evaluating the company's internal and external environment to determine its current position and potential for future growth. The internal factors (strengths and weaknesses) relate to Sonoran's resources, capabilities, infrastructure, and core competencies. The external factors (opportunities and threats) relate to the federal budget, needs of the federal government with respect to contracted professional services, and the competition.

The key to a successful SWOT analysis is to be truthful to yourself when you are doing it. I suggest having someone you trust and respect to help you with the SWOT analysis, if possible, in order to avoid personal biases.

For example, consider the operations of a food catering business during the COVID-19 pandemic. What were the catering business's strengths? What were the weaknesses and opportunities? What were the threats? If you owned a catering business, your business probably experienced several unpleasant realities. First, key revenue generating events such as weddings, retirement parties, graduations, and family reunions etc. were cancelled or postponed. The pandemic was a major threat that exposed a weakness your catering business probably realized, but not to the depth and impact in had on your bottom line. Simply put, a catering business is heavily dependent on in-person gatherings.

Second, for a certain segment of the catering industry, the pandemic brought about new opportunities, like food trucks. No doubt food trucks were making a slow but steady comeback in certain urban areas before the pandemic, but the post-pandemic era definitely gave food trucks a big boost. Today, the catering industry doesn't have to have in-person gatherings in order to generate revenue. Businesses can create and prepare great-tasting food (your main strength) and bring it to your customers.

Some final thoughts on SWOT. As a business owner, an advisor may tell you to prepare a ten-year business plan. While your ten-year plan might be strategic in nature, there's about three years of reality to it. Because the world changes rapidly, your well thought out ten-year business plan will probably become obsolete before you know it. However, if you had a three-year plan, the timeline for execution is faster and more agile for rapid change. In other words, you will be better prepared for unexpected circumstances. Similarly, we can do this on a personal level. What are your personal strengths, your weaknesses, opportunities to gain experience and develop, and the threats against you? Bottom line, be prepared to accept, and overcome the obstacles in your life because every leader will eventually encounter them.

Business Financial Sustainability

At our highest point at Sonoran Technology, we had around 350 employees working in 27 states. We grew so big, in fact, that we grew out of the small business category in terms of annual revenue. Our graduation from a small business to a large business took us out of our niche market (aircrew training) and changed the competition landscape. As a result, we had fewer contracting opportunities to bid on and our employee numbers decreased as the previously awarded contracts ended. If there was a positive outcome to successfully growing Sonoran Technology, and then seeing the company downsize, it was that we saw it coming and prepared accordingly. My primary concern at the time was to maintain our corporate staff and our corporate infrastructure levels. Instead of having the corporate staff take a pay cut or have a reduction in staff, I took a huge pay cut. You could say I went part-time in terms of pay, but the number of hours I worked increased. Some would call it a personal sacrifice, but for me it was a simple business decision, nothing more.

During this downsizing period, we went from being a prime contractor to being a highly sought after teaming partner or subcontractor. We cut a few corners here and there in order to remain profitable and maintain our line of credit with the bank. After being on the small business sidelines for four years, on January 1, 2023, Sonoran reentered our small business niche markets as a prime contractor! This is an example not about me, but rather our corporate leadership team making smart business decisions versus making unwise money decisions. For the team, they knew if there was a pay cut to be made, I would be the first person to take a pay cut.

This is a leadership example of putting your money where your heart is, not where your mouth is. This is how you grow your character credit score.

Your business' financial stability is also stability for your employees and serves as a key component for life-change. To do that, you need to have the foresight as a leader to have a plan in place. Using your banking relationships, you can secure funding and resources before you need them. Your character credit score can avoid any missteps if you are proactive by having solutions to problems before they arise.

The founding pastor at Palm Valley Church, located in Goodyear, Arizona was fond of saying *"People get funny when you mess with their money."* Kind of corny, yes. Is it true? You would be wise to believe it and honor it.

Let us say for example, your business has been up and running for one year. Congratulations! The question is, do you have reasonable revenue and profits to continue operations for another year? If not, borrowing money to run "day-to-day operations" does not solve your problem. It will only add debt to your business' P&L (profit and loss) statement. It's one thing to have capital to start a small business, it is another to have sufficient operating capital to stay in business.

There are a couple of examples, particularly in the federal contracting market space that showcase the need for financial insight and wisdom. Here is a real-life financial scenario for a small business working in the federal contracting market. Your company wins a federal contract with the Department of Transportation, and the contract starts officially on June 1st. Normally the terms of payment are Net 30, which means you should probably get paid approximately thirty days after the Government receives your invoice. Realistically speaking, from June 1st to the 30th, your business has performed the work, but you have not received a dime because you just submitted your first invoice to the government on July 1st.

When the invoice processing system is working, it normally takes 30 days to receive payment for the services you delivered in June. Most state law requires the employer to make payroll no later than 10 days after the first payroll period ended. This could mean, depending on the state your business is registered in, the payday for your employees performed from June 1st to

June 15th is June 25th. Your next payday is on or about July 10th for the work performed from June 16th to June 30th. That means there is a strong likelihood your business needs capital to cover three pay periods before the business receives payment on your first invoice. Once again, *"people get funny when you mess with their money."* The moral of the story is you need to have adequate capital to stay in business.

We Live in this Box Called Time

As a small business owner, it is common to work a lot of hours. When you are first starting out that could mean twelve, thirteen, or fourteen hours a day, whatever it takes to get the job done.

When the sun goes down, you take a break, see your significant other, the kids, and you are done for the day. You should never work yourself into oblivion because if you are not healthy mentally, physically, and spiritually, who is going to lead your business? Small business owners need to know when it is time to take a breather, a break, or even a nap. The reality is, the sun is going to come up, and you will see a new day.

The point here is balance. In order to be your best, business owners must have balance in their lives; physical, emotional, nutritional, and spiritual. In today's fast paced world, the major culprit is the lack of sleep. Neglecting yourself, family, friends, and other things in life that are important to you is a path to unimaginable stress and eventually burnout. For me, Fridays after twelve noon is my time. I turn off the cellphone and laptop computer and I normally go to the movies. I say, "Don't call me, I'm done for the day." The corporate staff, friends, and business colleagues know and respect the fact that I am PTO (personal time off) even though I didn't leave town.

In today's world, for most small business owners, we live in this box called time. If you opened the calendar on my cellphone, you could pull up my meetings and activities for the rest of the month and probably for a couple of months out. When you are running a business, it is understandable that your time is really important. However, we have only so much time in this box called life.

Unfortunately, none of us really knows how much time is remaining in our individual boxes. But here is what I do know; when you take some time out to give it to somebody or something, you are not getting it back. The old business saying "time is money" is over simplified. For me time is life.

When I spend time helping and mentoring a new business owner or entrepreneur, that is time I'm not going to get back. If it is time well spent, I am happy about that. Time wasted, however, is a recipe to make somebody unhappy because of what else they could have spent their valuable time—like helping the neighbor or having dinner with a friend or family. People are more conscious of their time and how it is being used now more than ever. Protect your time and protect others' time because it is one of the most important commodities you have. Be careful how you use your time and learn to say no when the time is likely to be wasted.

CHAPTER 5 TAKEAWAYS

- Whether you are a small business with five or 125 employees, regularly scheduled leadership meetings, in-person or virtual, are a policy that will improve communications at all levels of your business.

- Sending texts or emails does not ensure everyone reads it or fully understands what you were trying to convey.

- The business owner who thinks they can do it all is going to have a tough time leading and running their business.

- The wise leader carefully assesses the situation. Listen to what is and what is **not** being said.

- A good rule of thumb when it comes to financial stability is to access capital before you need it.

- A SWOT analysis (strength, weakness, opportunity, and threat) is a strategic planning tool that helps individuals and organizations identify their strengths, weaknesses, opportunities, and threats.

- You cannot work yourself into oblivion because if you are not healthy mentally, physically, and spiritually, who is going to lead your business?

Consistently Engaging Your Employees

Take Care of Employees to Take Care of the Customer

What or who makes your business go?

The people. Without people you do not have a company.

I do not know of any company that does not rely on its people in order to function effectively. This might sound obvious or overstated but businesses that don't put emphasis on the people are probably the ones that are mediocre, or that are on the road to closure. At Sonoran Technology, technically on paper we train pilots and aircrews. As a business owner, though, I consider us as a company in the people business. People are the most important assets to your company. Now, I do not like calling people tools or assets or commodities, because to me, it devalues them. However, it is true, your employees are the engine and energy that makes your company go! As a business owner, you must lead from that perspective.

I find it interesting that people who have similar life stories, oftentimes appreciate what you are trying to do or have done. Your journey somehow resonates with their journey, and they develop a special place in their heart because they understand what you're going through.

This is something I noticed when I was an adjunct at Arizona

State University (ASU) West Valley Campus teaching in the evening graduate and undergraduate programs. A lot of my students were working adults who were taking evening classes in pursuit of a bachelor's or master's degree. I recognized the students were in a similar position to me when I was going to college at night.

As their professor, I was not lenient or easy on them. The ASU academic standard was the standard they were held to. However, I understood their situation. On the first night of class I let it be known that "if you have a kid at home with a 102 fever, please, don't come to class. Take care of the family first. We will work our way through the reading assignments."

"Family first" is a leadership value that is priceless. It unequivocally says what you value as a leader, a business owner, and as human being. When your business is known for "taking care of its employees," believe me, the word gets around and before you know it, people will come knocking at your door. Relationships! It's all about relationships.

One of the most important human interaction distinctions is the difference between leading and managing. You cannot lead the chair you're sitting in because it is an inanimate object. The same goes for people; you can't treat people like equipment. We can manage equipment like a chair to make sure it is functioning, that the wheels are working, and that the chair moves back and forth and is in operating condition. However, it is impossible to lead or influence this inanimate object to do anything. People, while they can be managed, are more powerful if they are inspired and motivated. Inspirational leadership seeks to draw the most out of people. Lead what breathes!

Often as business owners we put a great deal of emphasis on

our customers. Yes, we must take care of the customer. However, there is another step before that—engaging our employees. You know, the folks that are front and center; the ones who actually service your customers. When the employees are happy, satisfied, engaged, valued, and respected, they pass those same sentiments on to the customer.

It's important to emphasize to your employees that they are important individuals and a part of any success your business experiences. When there's a weak link in the chain, the entire business leadership chain is weaker. I will give an example. Consider the person who is in charge of payroll. Twice a month, they are the most important people in the company. They are in fact the captain of the ship on payroll day. If that person feels insignificant when payroll is not front and center, chances are there is a problem brewing.

If any employee thinks their role in the company is insignificant, then that's the business owner's fault. It is our fault, and it is on us to fix it immediately. It's imperative your employees understand they are appreciated and add value to the company. If an employee feels and believes they are there just for a paycheck, chances are you are not getting their best effort. Either you hired the wrong person, or there is something in your company's culture that needs an adjustment.

There are a multitude of reasons people change jobs. It could be inadequate pay and benefit, a long commute, or maybe the job wasn't what they thought it would be, or the right fit for them. The employee Sonoran looks for goes beyond their resume. We look for people who want to be a part of something greater than themselves. People who want to grow in all aspects of their lives. Why? Because I believe humans naturally gravitate to leaders and organizations that will bring out the best of us. Which brings me to the question, does your company have a leadership development program? How much time do you spend developing leaders from within your company?

When I graduated from the Air Force Fighter Weapons School located at Nellis Air Force Base Nevada in October 1987, the school's objective was to go back to send graduates back to our home units to teach squadron instructors and ensure the squadron was combat ready! Additionally, as Weapons School graduates, we were responsible for identifying and grooming the next Weapons School student candidates. Bottom line, the Air Force's Weapons School is purposely designed to train and equip leaders.

As a business owner, it is highly recommended that you have a deliberate plan when you are looking to select and develop the next leader in your company. Do you know who your high potential and next leaders are? What are you doing to mentor and groom them?

Your Communication Style Matters

Your communication style will have an enormous impact on how you engage with your employees. When you think about how the business world has changed over the past twenty-five years or so in terms of technology, social media, generational demographics, and multifaceted work environments, chances are the way we used to communicate needs updating. To a certain degree, our professional communication styles are modeled after our personal communication preferences. One example of how personal and professional communications overlap is what I call "marriage communication syndrome," a nice way of saying one of us is not hearing.

My wife will tell me, "You hate to be wrong." I respond by telling her "Maybe you did not hear exactly what I said." In the marriage communication syndrome, Malinda will tell me I said something, and I will deny it because I know those words are not in my vocabulary. The marriage communication syndrome is best summed up as "you heard what you thought I said, so we have to let it go and agree to disagree."

The marriage communication syndrome highlights miscommunication between logical and emotional individuals. Logic are the words that were said, or we thought were said, while an emotional part is how the words are received or interpreted. If you are not careful, it can quickly become your company's communication syndrome. As business owners, we need to be precise and unambiguous in all mediums of communication. Moreover, our communications need to be simple and meaningful: message sent, message received, and message interpreted as intended.

As communication modalities evolve, you may want to consider having a communications policy or guidelines for your business, especially when it comes to protecting proprietary data and information. If you decide to establish communication protocols for your business, you can start by asking your employees to answer a few questions. These questions are designed to see how they view certain types and communications and what their preferences are:

- What is the purpose of a text message?
- How long should an email be?

- What should not be in an email or text message?
- What is the purpose of the cc: and bcc: threads?
- What is your preferred communication method?

For me, I view text messages as a means for passing along simple information, or data. The senior staff know that if someone sends me a long text, chances are I will call that individual and have a discussion, politely ask them not to send me lengthy text or emails and explain why. Emails, especially. There are not enough pages to discuss the pros, cons, and consequences of emails. At Sonoran we established a very simple principle when it comes to email communications: "Before you hit send on an email or text, imagine that email being in a courtroom on a big screen."

I learned the value of this lesson about 20 years ago. We had an aircrew training contract and the contract's program manager was a good friend of mine. We were crew members during our active-duty days. This was a new contract and he and I were looking for a team of specialized former Air Force mission crew instructors. The company we worked for had a couple of part-time recruiters at corporate who had never served in the military. The corporate recruiters did not know the military lingo, they did not have the credentials to access any of the local military installations to attend job fairs, and they did not know the Air Force culture. The program manager who reported to me was the first in line to review the resumes of potential hires. I could sense he was becoming frustrated and outright upset with the quality of candidates he was receiving.

One day I received an email from him saying "Paul, the recruiters at the corporation are incompetent. They are sending me resumes of people who are unqualified. We should take them out back and..." You get the point. I completely understood his frustration because the company's recruiting process was severely broken, and this was not the first time we had experienced this nightmare scenario.

The only problem with his email reply was he pushed the *"reply all"* button on his computer keyboard. Everyone in the corporate HR branch, recruiters, the HR vice president, and my boss who was a vice president of operations, all were addressees. There is an obvious lesson to be learned here that is worth repeating: "Before you hit the send button on any kind of electronic communication device, visualize your message on a large screen in a courtroom."

As your business grows, so must your internal and external communication plan. The more generationally diverse your workforce becomes, the more you must monitor your company's culture. As an example, many people in the 20–40 year-old age range have become so familiar with text messaging as their preferred medium they see phone calls as an intrusion unless permission is granted via text. I found this astonishing as my preferred method is to actually pick up the phone. Focusing on effective communication and employee engagement will allow us to create a tapestry of talent with different ideas, different values, and diverse cultures.

Responsibility vs Accountability

I am responsible for my own actions. I am accountable to my family, and I am accountable to my faith.

I don't know how the exit interview is going to go at the end of my life. I imagine myself standing there before God, and He says, "I know what you did, but I want to hear from you. What did you do with all the gifts and talents I blessed you with? Did you use them for yourself, or did you share those with others?" As faith based believers, we have gifts and talents. Even before this book was published, I had already begun thinking about what portions of the proceeds from the book sales will go straight to helping others and to various non-profit organizations. Bottom line is that I truly believe we are blessed to be a blessing to others. I am blessed with certain business and leadership skills that I enjoy sharing with others. That is something for which I am accountable. The decision of what I do with my talents and blessings, is all mine.

While we can delegate responsibilities, we cannot delegate accountability. What that means is we as business owners and leaders are ultimately accountable for our company's outcomes and performance. I had a situation where Sonoran had six people on an Army contract, and one was a real problem.

The problem employee was good at his job, but people hated collaborating with this person. The employee had a unique skill set that was in high demand at the time. During one of my site visits, the program manager told me he had documented the employee's unprofessional behavior twice in the past six months. Fortunately for the employee, he had scheduled vacation time during my visit. As I always do when visiting a site, I took the team out to lunch. I asked the team how things were going, and they all bemoaned the unprofessional attitude of the employee on vacation.

I asked if they would be willing to work a few extra hours a day until we found a replacement. They all gladly said they would work the extra time in exchange for not working with the problem employee. That is a sign of how bad this person was to work with.

The site manager or program manager at any Sonoran job site is responsible for getting the team to function as a cohesive unit. The manager is ultimately responsible for getting the job done. The manager is also responsible for making sure that the customer is happy and satisfied. However, when things "go south" or when things go badly, all accountability goes back to the business owner—me and you. Ultimately, we are accountable for everything that happens in our business. This "wrong fit" employee was a distraction to the company. He was a distraction to the team. And since we as business owners are accountable for what happens in the company, we are also responsible for firing bad employees. We cannot delegate accountability.

Put Your Money Where Your Heart Is

Genuine enthusiasm, loyalty, kindness, and honesty is contagious.

One of our employees had a brand-new baby. The baby is doing fine, the parents are elated, and life is grand. A few weeks later, our HR manager was told that our newest little Sonoran family member has been having serious medical problems. Our employee, whose family is still connected with the military, were told the baby need to fly to an Air Force Hospital immediately. There is only one problem, our employee didn't have any vacation time in the books. As owner and president of Sonoran, I had several options at my disposal. The HR manager and I could send an email out to the entire company and ask for vacation time donations. We could have given our employee advanced vacation time, or reach into my personal vacation bucket, which is unlimited. You see, I know this family personally, and I also understand not having a salary for a week or two could cause financial hardship.

In discussion with the chief financial officer and HR manager, we decided to advance the employee one week of vacation in addition to donating two weeks of vacation from my bucket. The goal was simple, alleviate the family's money concerns so they could focus on the baby health. The reason for our actions were plain and simple: It was the right thing to do, and we had the resources to do it.

Several years ago, we had a similar situation where one of our employees experienced a serious medical incident that resulted in a long-term disability. This time we sent an email asking if Sonoran family members would donate vacation time. In just a few days our employees across the country **donated over 450 hours of vacation time.** Wow! To me this said a lot about Sonoran's culture and more about this amazing group of top-notch professionals respectfully known as the Sonoran Family.

The lesson here: put your money where your heart is. Can we do that every time and without someone taking advantage of our generosity? Probably not, but these kinds of medical emergencies don't happen very often so it's not a big deal.

I was told once by a former Sonoran program manager that his paycheck was his "certificate of appreciation." In other words, you can show your employees that you appreciate them in a lot of different ways, but the most impactful way is a competitive salary, great fringe benefits, and human dignity through respect.

We value and appreciate the work our employees do, and so does our customers. The business owner's goal should be to compensate them you as best you can. Another way we show appreciation is go the extra mile with thank you letters, birthday cards, performance bonuses, social events and consistently being there for them and their families.

When I was 20 years old, my first overseas assignment was in the Republic of South Korea capital, Seoul. I was the youngest and lowest ranking person in the Air Force Office of Special Investigations (AFOSI) unit. This was a one-year remote tour that escalated my maturity as a young man more than I ever expected. All the people in the unit, both officers and non-commissioned officers, looked out for me and made sure I stayed on the right track. This probably had a lot to do with our commander, Colonel Whiteside, and his leadership and the high expectations he set for everyone under his command.

Fast forward six years later. I'm now a captain in the Air Force stationed at Luke Air Force Base in Arizona. While visiting my parents in Mississippi, my mom asks, "Did I ever show you the letter your commander in Korea sent me and your dad?" I was confused. "What letter?" I asked. Mom reached into her Bible and pulled out this letter worn and faded letter she had been saving. In the letter was a picture of me receiving my third stripe (promotion to E-4), with my Commander and immediate supervisor Chief Cantu. The letter read: "Dear Mr. & Mrs. Smiley, today we celebrated Paul's 20th birthday. He is doing very well over here. He has enormous potential, he is always courteous, and does an excellent job. I guarantee you we will send him back home safely." The letter was signed by Colonel Whiteside.

I never knew this letter existed. After reading it, I was overcome with emotion as I realized how much the commander, my supervisors, and all the unit members cared about me. Later in my career, as a squadron Commander I told the First Sergeant, "Buy a camera. Every time one of our young airmen receives a promotion or special award, we are going capture the moment and send their families the picture and a hand-written note from both of us." The unintentional leadership lesson I learned from Colonel Whiteside was timeless and has never escaped me. The Colonel, and so many others along my life journey, helped shape my leadership style which is centered around showing people you care. In doing so, the people you are leading will learn to replicate it as well.

CHAPTER 6 TAKEAWAYS

- What or who makes your business go? The people. Without people, you do not have company.

- It is important to emphasize to your employees that they are important and a part of any success the business experiences.

- Not only is communication important, but your communication style will also have an enormous impact on how you engage with your employees.

- As your business grows, so must your internal and external communication plan.

- While we can delegate responsibilities, we cannot delegate accountability.

- Genuine enthusiasm, loyalty, kindness, and honesty is contagious.

- Continuously show your employees and customers that you care!

Getting to Know Your Customers Better

Serve + Us = Service

Customers believe our job is to serve them. As business owners our job is to provide the best service possible, regardless of the kind of business you operate.

Although we do not talk about it a lot, there are difficult customers; these are the customers you just do not want.

A few years ago, I was at the local dry cleaners where I've been a customer for the last 20 years. The gentleman who owns the cleaners is a very nice guy, soft spoken, respectful, courteous, and will always go the extra mile to make his customers happy. One day I was at his store picking up an order. There was a customer in front of me who was picking up a wedding dress, and she was arguing that a stain on it could not come out.

The owner explained as best he could that he tried everything possible, but the stain on the dress would not come out.

"Well, you have to try harder!" she yelled back. "And by the way, the little clamps got bent, too!"

There was about 20 minutes of this back and forth before she finally left the store.

The owner smiled at me, and asked me, "Well Colonel Smiley, what would you do?" I told him, "There are some customers you just do not want. Those kinds of customers are just too painful to work with." Here is a question: If you were the owner of this company, what would you have said to the customer? If it were me, I would have said: "I am sorry. There is no charge. We tried our very best to fix it, but maybe somebody else can help you."

As business owners it is up to up to us to make sure that the customers we have are the customers we want. I'm sure there are some business owners who would argue this point. One could argue "It's revenue, why would you turn down revenue and lose a customer?"

My response is in the form of a question. Are you making a business decision or money decision?

Case and point, sometimes when I buy a car, there is a 50/50 chance I will get the inexperienced salesperson. After buying cars for over 45 years, for me, the difference between an experienced and an inexperienced salesperson is the kinds of questions they ask. So, depending on their questions, a relationship of some sort is being formed. It's either going to be a win-win or win-lose transaction.

The point is, in addition to selling a product or service, your business should also be trying to form a long-term business relationship. What you want is a customer to walk away and tell their friends, "Wow I had such a great experience with/at (your business)!"

While stationed in Las Vegas I was referred to as a Honda dealer by my friend. When we finally decided to buy a Honda Accord a few months later, my friend told me "Be sure to ask for, Nico. He's the blond-haired guy with a ponytail." When I arrived at the dealership, I asked for Nico. Nico came out, I told him exactly what I was looking for, model, color, configuration, how much I was willing to spend, and that we only had 45 minutes.

Long story short, I was in and out of the dealership in less than one hour. A few months later someone asked me "Where did you buy your Honda?" I said go to the Honda dealership downtown and ask for Nico. Remember, great customer service and great relationships sell themselves. Conversely, a reputation of poor customer service and bad relationships spreads even faster. It is a two-way street.

Delivering exceptional customer service starts with being a good customer yourself. When someone provides good or above average service, I earnestly and sincerely thank them, and if the opportunity presents itself, I make the extra effort to let the manager know that the person(s) that served me was outstanding. Just because we are receiving a service, the serve-us part does not mean we shouldn't also be nice, friendly, and encouraging. You never know what impact a kind word can do for someone who is doing their best but is still having a bad day.

In a competitive market, customers have options and will choose to do business with the companies that provide the best experience. It is important for businesses to prioritize customer satisfaction in order to grow their customer base, grow the business, and stay ahead of the competition. Business leaders can take better care of customers by gathering and acting on customer feedback.

First, we must provide opportunities for customers to give feedback and make their voices heard. Gathering feedback through formal channels (customer service surveys, online surveys, or social media) or informal channels are equally valuable. Question—how does it make you feel when the chef or the restaurant manager stops by your table and asks, "How is everything?" The simple fact that someone cares is always a positive feeling.

Once the feedback is collected, you can integrate customer feedback into decision-making processes and use customer feedback to drive innovation, fix problems, and improve customer satisfaction. This process creates a feedback loop to continually improve the customer's experience.

Several years ago, a small city in the southwest suburbs of Phoenix, Arizona, conducted an online survey of its residents "What businesses are we missing?" The citizens responded by saying, "The city needs an organic grocery store, a brewery style restaurant, and an upscale restaurant." The last I heard, that city is in negotiations to bring in those and many more stores and restaurants as part of its strategic growth plan. The result is the citizens felt the city leaders heard and appreciated their feedback. That is my kind of town, a town that listens to its residents.

Finally, there's a cautionary tale to be considered when it comes to customer feedback and surveys. Surveys can sometimes be perceived as intrusive and time consuming. In a world of unprecedented cybersecurity attacks, consumers are becoming more vigilant when it comes to sharing their personal information and responding to electronic surveys.

Successful business owners are usually visionaries in their respective markets. They see possibilities and future opportunities where others only see the here and now. The visionary business owner is not overly concerned with immediate profits because they are in what I call the "seed planting mode." They understand the best path to a plentiful harvest is to plant seeds which is a building block for future opportunities, business growth, brand recognition, and relationships.

The Art of Grace in Customer Relationships

If I had to pick one word that really defines a great small business with servant leaders, outstanding employees, and loyal customers, that word would be grace.

Grace is important in customer relationships because it helps to create a positive experience for the customer and builds trust and loyalty. We can show grace in customer relationships by understanding and empathizing with the customer's needs and concerns. We can provide extra assistance or accommodation. We under promise and over deliver. We acknowledge and apologize for any shortcomings or missteps. Moreover, we show genuine interest and care for the customer's well-being and demonstrate a willingness to make things right. Grace in customer relationships helps to build strong and lasting relationships, cement customer loyalty, and promote positive word-of-mouth.

I have been a long-term customer with a certain carpet and tile cleaning company for over 20 years. The company's customer service is always above average, and their employees are smart, experienced, and considerate of my time. The only thing I did not like was the four-hour service window. This is their arrival time, not the time to service your home.

But things have changed at this company. They developed a phone application that allows their customers to track where the service technician is and provides regulars updates. For me this was a game changer. I could now leave the house and do other things because, let us face it, no one, absolutely no one, likes sitting at home waiting for a service call.

A single experience of grace, or lack thereof, paints a picture of how your entire relationship with this business will go.

Several years ago, my wife picked out and pre-ordered a truck from a dealership. When we went to pick up her truck in July, I asked the sales representative "Do you have any water?" They pointed me to the vending machine, where I'd have to buy my own water.

The sale representative did not say "No problem; let me go get you a couple of bottles of water." It was July in Arizona. We spend over thirty thousand dollars with that dealership, and they can't offer their customer two bottles of water? I told my wife "If we hadn't already paid for this truck, I would have walked out of that dealership." Sure, it was just water, but it clearly demonstrated what we could expect from the dealership's service or parts department if we had a problem in the future.

There are several possibilities here. Maybe the dealership didn't value or understand customer-centered grace. Perhaps the dealership didn't hire or train their sales representatives properly. Maybe the dealership's motto was to make as much money as you can; remember, most car salespeople work on commission. Either way, it is the business owner who is ultimately accountable for the customer's experience. In the end, the only thing I know for sure is, they will never get my business again. Sound familiar?

Knowing What Your Customers Want

About 17 years ago, I was in L.A. at an event called the Diversity Suppliers Annual Gathering. There were about 3,000 people at the event, and the guest speaker was basketball legend, NBA Hall of Famer, and mega entrepreneur Earvin "Magic" Johnson Jr.

A few weeks before the event, Mr. Johnson had just opened

several Magic Johnson Theaters in an African American dominated area in Los Angeles. In his speech, he noted that on the first weekend opening, a couple of theaters ran out of hot dogs.

"Why did that happen?" he asked. "I'll tell you why that happened," he said. "My vendors for the theaters didn't know my people—Black people."

Mr. Johnson continued by saying "Black people don't do dinner and a movie; they have dinner at the movies."

Mr. Johnson's point was his vendors did not know or understand his customers, and in the end, that is why his team did not have enough hot dogs. Mr. Johnson offered another example of knowing what the customer wants. "I have several Starbucks coffee shops in this same L.A. area. If you went to one of my Starbucks coffee shops, you would not see us selling scones. Scones are not popular with most Black people. Instead, we sell bear claws and red velvet cake."

It was a direct and non-apologetic bluster that resonated with me.

Although it was the vendors who fell short that opening weekend, as the owner, Mr. Johnson took full responsibility, and clearly explained why it happened. He knew, and so did everyone at the conference, that leaders must better understand and serve their customers.

The United Services Automobile Association, better known by their acronym USAA, is an excellent example for providing exceptional customer service. While there are competitors who can beat their price, remember the question that a lot of USAA members and I ask is, "can the competitors beat their service?" Again, that is when it all comes full circle for most customers;

serve + us = service. Their tagline reflects that, "Members first, mission always."

A dear and close friend and I attend the same church. He is an Air Force retiree and has a small business installing home entertainment and security systems. He installed a state-of-the-art system in our home which cost $7,500. Sticker shock, yes, but it was well worth it. When I paid him, I said "That was an expensive project. Is that the going rate?" I then realized; this was an opportunity to explain to him this concept of customer grace.

I suggested that he should do something to express to his customers that he deeply appreciated their business, their trust in him, and that if they had any problems his company would be there for them. I said, "I'm not sure what your profit margin is on this deal, but, if you send me a $50 gift card, or a coffee mug, or something to remind your customer of the relationship you are trying to build, it could make a huge difference." He followed through and sent me a small model airplane for my office. Now, every time I see the Air Force airplane, I think of the magnificent work he did at our home. It is a similar process when you purchase a home, the real estate agent or home builder always gives you a gift of some kind. My friend has adopted this customer appreciation model and today, his customer base is growing steadily.

When I fly, I fly Delta Airlines 99% of the time. The reason is simple— exceptional customer service from start to finish. After every trip there is a Delta email that reads, "Paul, thank you for your business." And when something on the trip goes wrong, like a two-hour flight delay, etc., they acknowledge and will try to incentivize me on the next trip. As a small business owner, how do you acknowledge your customers?

My barber, who I have had for over 20 years, always has a gift for me at Christmas time. It can be something as simple as a personalized Christmas card. Stamped Christmas cards with automatic labeling doesn't do the trick. Ultimately, the companies that have the best understanding of service, grace, and do the due diligence to better know their customers, stand to gain the most.

CHAPTER 7 TAKEAWAYS

- As business owners it is up to us to make sure that the customer you have is the customer that you want.

- Great customer service and great relationships sell themselves.

- Delivering exceptional customer service starts with being a good customer yourself.

- In a competitive market, customers have options and will choose to do business with the companies that provide the best experience.

- Grace is important in customer relationships because it helps to create a positive experience for the customer and builds trust and loyalty.

- When it all comes full circle for most customers, serve + us = service.

CHAPTER 8

Observe the Competition

Starbucks or Dutch Bros?

Recently, during one of the SBA sponsored *Boots to Business* seminars I asked the question, "Who here likes Starbucks, and who likes Dutch Bros?" Dutch Bros is a popular coffee chain in the western U.S. known for their bubbly staff, fun music, and espresso drinks. Starbucks is well, Starbucks is well, Starbucks, a well-known, respected, and industry giant.

The result was a 50/50 split for either brand.

I started asking the audience to tell me why they liked Starbucks or Dutch Bros. Most of the responses were similar. Starbucks fans said Dutch Bros staff talk too much; I just want my coffee. Dutch Bros drinkers said they liked the community and enjoyed the friendliness of the staff. The interesting takeaway front this training session was that **nobody talked about the coffee.**

Nobody talked about the product. Nobody said they preferred one menu over the other, or the taste, or even the price. They all focused on personal experience and not the actual drinks they were buying.

Dutch Bros storefronts are typically small drive through locations with some patio seating. Starbucks, meanwhile, all have tables and chairs to work or hangout at. Starbucks has also evolved as a place for social relationships. If you want to sit down and relax, go to Starbucks. If you want to grab a drink and have some high energy conversation, go to Dutch Bros. They are two completely different business models serving two different customer markets.

Just as every customer is not the ideal customer for your business, the same goes for employees. This ties back to hiring the "right fit" talent. Disney sells happiness so they hire happy people. Dutch Bros sells high energy and friendliness, so they hire bubbly people. A Dutch Bros employee will not necessarily make a good Starbucks employee and vice versa. While they are both baristas, they are not the same *brand* of barista.

The current competitive environment is people. Every time you train someone, and someone leaves you, it leaves a hole in your team and could impact customer service. So, while companies are continuously competing for customers, they are also competing for great employees. One way of observing the competition is to monitor how they are not only attracting but *hiring and retaining* the top talent. What are their selling points? Is it their company culture, competitive compensation and benefits, promotion opportunities for growth and advancement, or simply your competitor's brand?

Observe the competition and recognize it is still about the key principles in the *Smiley Leadership and Mentoring Experience*. Putting people before profit can get you further in your industry. Remember, when I asked them which coffee place they preferred, nobody talked about the coffee.

Being Your Own Leader and Business

"There are different kinds of gifts, but the same Spirit distributes them. 5 There are different kinds of service, but the same Lord. 6 There are different kinds of working, but in all of them and in everyone it is the same God at work"

– 1 Corinthians 12:4-6[27]

This passage from the Bible celebrates our differences and the diversity of gifts, service, and working that exist among individuals. It highlights that despite these differences, it is the same God who works in and through each person. Yet, our differences are what make us all unique.

When it comes to competition, the key words are respect and understanding. When you respect and understand that your competition is just a different blessing your faith is giving you, you realize competition is not a bad thing. Competition is a good thing. Personally, Sonoran Technology is not worried about competing with Boeing, Lockheed Martin, or any large aircraft defense industry company. These companies are out of Sonoran Technology's league in more ways than one. I have seen several small business owners struggle with trying to get on the large business stage because they want to be viewed as one of the big players. These small businesses are trying to take on a big business mantra that simply does not fit the small business profile. Instead, if they embraced their uniqueness, and didn't focus on being something they are not, they would have a better chance of sustained growth and success.

Understanding and operating in the lane that best fits what you do best is an important element of knowing your competition. The only thing you need to do is strive to be the best you can be in your respective lane. Just like Starbucks and Dutch Bros, they purposefully stay in their lanes. What drives choice can be seen from the customer's viewpoint. Customers like competition because it gives them more choices. Sometimes, they choose a business that offers the lowest price; but you get what you pay for. There are other times the customer chooses the business that is most dependable. And when it comes to retaining customers, stay in your lane. If you are good at what you do, and you are known and respected for your "exceptionalism," customers will find you.

Using a Sonoran example, when a federal government releases a request for proposal (RFP), the Government contracting office will tell you what they want to see in terms of technical solutions, past performance history, and price.

It's up to each company (bidder) to not only provide the Government with a low risk solution, but also convince the Government that your company's solution is the best amongst the competition. Considering all aspects of the RFP and allocating proposal resource dollars, smart and experienced companies will ask the all-important question—what are the chances of us winning the contract? Companies that have been around for a while usually have a good sense about the competition. In the federal contracting market, just like the local lottery, you cannot win if you do not play.

In any competitive market, it's important to understand the only thing that you have control over is consistently delivering the best customer products, services, and experiences possible. Some companies will say their product is "the best on the market" or "their product offers the best value and price." Whether your competition's product lives up to its billing is for the customer to decide, not you. I firmly believe it's the customer experience that keeps them coming back or moving on to your competitors. After all, one of the tenable principles of doing business is only doing business with people you trust.

Separating Winning from Losing

Are you a competitive person?

I would say I am not a competitive person. I'm not competitive in the way that Michael Jordan is said to be "fueled by his desire to win." Winning for me has a different meaning than most other folks. I think you can win even when you lose because there's are valuable lessons to be learned.

This philosophy goes back to my faith. If Sonoran is what the Government deems an "unsuccessful bidder" when we bid on a Government contract, we don't have a pity party.

We accept the results, determine why we were not the winning company, document the lessons learned, and move on to the next opportunity. That is one perspective. It could be that the winning company simply submitted a better proposal.

I try to understand outcomes from an inner perspective. While no business owner likes losing, we clearly understand and accept the fact our company will not win every contract we bid for. From 2011 to 2017, Sonoran had a major winning streak as a prime contractor. Our efforts to remain a low-profile, under the radar small business didn't last long, because when you're winning multi-million-dollar contracts time and time again, believe me, your competition takes notice. At one point, our industry competitors considered Sonoran as "the one to beat."

Here's a cautionary tale; If you and your team are overly competitive, and just can't get over losing, it can become personal. It can slowly but surely weigh you down, and in the worst case can cloud your decision-making judgement. I've learned over the years that not winning a contract bid is never the end of the world. Success is not permanent, and failure is not fatal.

If I trust you and respect you, I do not consider you a competitor. You are simply the competition. What? Let me explain.

I know small business owners who I respect and trust even though we are in the same industry. They have won contracts where Sonoran was the competition. Sonoran's competition has also been unsuccessful in bidding on the contract that Sonoran won.

Admittedly, when the companies who I don't trust win, well, let us just say my feelings are not the same. These companies are our **competitors**, and they have a storied history of not playing fair and using revenge tactics. They have no conscience in falsely accusing a competitor company of misdeeds without losing any sleep. This is why I lived by my number one rule for conducting business: Only do business with people you trust. *No exceptions.*

There will always be competition and the chances are you will always have competitors.

Preserving Your Integrity in Competition

There is no winning that is worth the price of compromising your integrity.

In 1997, I was an Air Force Major assigned to the Joint Chiefs of Staff (JCS) at the Pentagon in Washington, DC. Our joint service team was tasked to go to, let's call it Country X, to meet with their Minister of Defense and Air Force leaders. Our Pentagon team consisted of twenty field grade officers from the U.S. Army, Navy, and Air Force. We were there to assess Country X's Air Defense capability due to their close proximity and ongoing threats from a neighboring adversary. The goal for Country X's Ministry of the Defense was to procure advanced military hardware from the United States.

We had two weeks to travel to various military bases within Country X and report our findings to a three-star general at the Pentagon. Overall, our team's findings were, let's say, average, in terms of Country X's ability to defend themselves from an attack. But there were political landmines our team chief had to maneuver through in in the Pentagon and in Congress. In the first version of our team's report, our assessment of the County X's air defenses was not what the Pentagon bosses had expected. Country X had problems and our team had lots of concerns.

We developed a stoplight rating system (red, yellow, and green) to show a visual depiction of our assessment of Country X's air defense capability. Red, of course meant things were bad. Yellow meant County X's air defense capabilities were satisfactory but needed equipment upgrades and additional operations training support. Green was the best rating and meant Country X could defend themselves. Bottom line, there was a mixture of red, yellow, and green stop lights in assessment. Our team chief knew he could not show our assessment chart to our top brass because military leaders from Country X's Ministry of Defense were scheduled to come to the Pentagon a few weeks later and our assessment could embarrass them. On the other hand, as military officers, my teammates and I would not lie about our findings, so we had to tell the truth in a more digestible way.

What we did was we added a fourth color, Blue to our stop light chart. Red was still bad, yellow was again satisfactory, the green rating definition remained the same, and the new blue rating really didn't mean anything, it just looked good at the time. It only symbolized where Country X wanted to go with future technological advances and arms sales. Our new and improved rating assessment rating chart told the same truth about Country X's military air defense capability without embarrassing our guests. What the top Pentagon brass seemed to forget was, Country X was not overly concerned about receiving blue ratings.

This high-level experience tested our team's integrity when it came to winning and losing. That is, winning or losing the trust and respect of our superior officers, and our Country X allies. As a small business owner, you may never be involved in decision makings conversations at the Pentagon level or working side-by-side with a major military power. But there will be instances where your integrity will be on the line, and what I suggest you do, is never sacrifice your integrity to win! You can be crafty and still win while operating within the rule book. Make no mistake about it, there was top-level pressure to get our team chief to change our assessment, but we did not.

Trust + Service = Satisfaction = Strong Relationships

If I trust you, and you are delivering what you promised, that makes a great relationship. Nowhere in that formula does it talk about price.

We all know we are paying a little bit more for good service, that's how the world operates. Take the cruise industry for example. There's Carnival cruises, and then there is Norwegian, Royal Caribbean, and other higher end cruise companies. A seasoned cruiser knows what to expect from each cruise line with respect to quality and customer service. Although a lot of the cruise lines are subsidiaries with one another, each has their own brand and customer demographics, and you get what you pay for.

Going back to USAA, their leadership and marketing team will tell you, "It's about the USAA experience." Through that experience customers learned what they value the most as USAA consumers. Not long ago, I received an email that said my automobile payment was overdue. This was confusing because all of my USAA policies are all set on autopay. I called their service desk and asked, "How is that possible with automatic payment?" She let me know the charge to my debit card was denied. I thought about it and remembered I had changed debit cards last month. "Oh, no problem. We can take care of that, thanks for letting us know!" I could tell she was smiling through the phone. It was a great customer service experience because while it was really my problem, USAA took ownership of my problem. Had it been an adversarial conversation, my demeanor and disposition, depending on whether the problem was solved, would have had an impact on the rest of my day. Also, on the same day, I was giving an important speech to a group of business owners. Because of how well USAA took care of me, my mind was free and clear when I showed up to the event. But because my interaction with USAA's "right fit" talent customer service professional exceeded my expectation, I was happy to share my experience with several friends during lunch.

Showing you care will help you and your company stand out from the competition. Take the opportunity to learn from every experience and transform losses into winning, learning experiences. Put people over profit and watch your business flourish.

CHAPTER 8 TAKEAWAYS

- One way of observing the competition is to monitor how they are not only attracting but hiring and retaining the top talent.

- Understanding and operating in the lane that best fits what you do best is an important element of knowing your competition.

- If you and your team are overly competitive, and just can't get over losing, it can become personal. It can slowly but surely weigh you down, and in the worst case can cloud your judgement.

- There is no winning that is worth the price of your integrity.

Seeking Value in the Struggle

Rebounding

> *"Consider it pure joy, my brothers and sisters, whenever you face trials of many kinds, because you know that the testing of your faith produces perseverance."*
>
> —*James 1:2-4*[28]

To show you the power of seeking value in the struggle, I want you to put yourselves in the shoes for this hypothetical scenario. Let's say you have demonstrated your leadership and business acumen, and you get introduced to a business owner that could use leadership experience and help with doing business with the federal government.

This business owner is one of those persons always looking for that fast-track, money-making opportunity. They had a great business opportunity, but you honestly believe they had no idea what they were doing.

Your first day on the job was unusual to say the least. The CEO of the bank that your new employer did business with sent over an auditor to perform a risk mitigation assessment. This is your first clue that there could be trouble. Having never owned a small business, you did not think too much of it at the time. Your job was to help the company win and manage contracts with the federal government. After about six months, it became obvious the owner was overly concerned with his six-figure salary and lavish lifestyle. One day the owner asked you to be the president of the company while they would take on the CEO role. This so-called sweet-sounding offer would have put you in harm's way with no parachute if the bottom fell out.

It would mean that you would be the company's president with no ownership in the company, and limited authority where things had to be cleared through the owner. For nearly 18 months, you gave it all you had.

You implemented new policies, procedures, business development processes, marketing strategies, and hired the best talent you could find. There was one missing piece—you did not have access to see the company's financials.

What do you do in this situation?

At one point, the owner asked you if you would loan them money to make the upcoming payroll. They told you the government was behind paying their invoices, which happens every now and then. So, you met with a finance lawyer who drew up a rock-solid promissory note to ensure you would be paid back with interest. Three months later as agreed to in the promissory note, you were paid in full.

Six months later, the CEO asked again if you could loan them money to make payroll. This time, you're being a lot more cautious. You thought to yourself, "wait a minute, the owner has a huge and expensive home and several fancy cars that they could either sell or put up as collateral." A few days later, the owner asked you to accompany them to a meeting with the company's banker. You're sitting in the bank VP's office. Your chair s positioned slightly behind the CEO, where you could see each other if you turned your heads. After the CEO stated their case as to why they needed a $500,000 line of credit, the bank VP professionally and politely said, "No. Your books are in shambles and my underwriters simply cannot follow the math. It appears your company is making lots of money, but we can't figure out where it's going."

As you were leaving the office, the bank VP silently mouthed to you "get out, leave the company as soon as you can."

Again, what do you do in this situation?

As you learn later, the CEO was receiving payment for the work the company had performed, but they weren't paying the bills. Instead, the owner paid themselves first, and whatever was leftover they paid the employees and vendors with. Their attitude was "if a vendor did not get paid, too bad."

Working with this CEO every day, you never saw or heard these feelings, but when it came to money, they were a different person. As it turns out, their personal finances were a disaster, and filing for bankruptcy was long overdue. During your time at the company, you could see the owner's stress levels almost explode right in front of you!

The banker told the owner, "I'm not loaning you $500,000 because I see how you take advantage of this situation." They were invoicing the government, but then did not pay any of the vendors once the company got paid.

There was one vendor who was owed close to one million dollars.

You say to the owner, "There's invoices from the government to cover this bill you have."

That's when the other shoe drops. The owner openly admitted that money had already been spent on other projects that were past due.

"What do you mean you already spent it?" you asked in disbelief. The business had people calling him and at the office and sending collection notices. The owner told the secretary not to take any calls or summons. They had so many vendors, lawyers, and lawsuits stacked up against them, you felt sorry for them and their family. The owner was trying to live in a lane of luxury that they simply could not afford, and it finally caught up with them.

It was not long after this that you tell the owner you're done. There was no way you could help them because the hole they had dug was too deep. When a bank auditor tells you that you are done, to close it down, and file for bankruptcy, you should probably take that advice! This business owner does not, and the rest is bad history.

Unbeknownst to you at that time, because you refused to loan the owner more money, they obtained money from a suspicious character. You find out later the new investor was charging them $2 for every $1 they borrowed. The hole got a lot deeper, and you realize you need to get your own parachute ready. So, you begin to make plans to start your own business, and you're sure to tell them about this new venture in writing so they could not come back later and accuse you of some nefarious activities.

Upon your departure, the CEO realized he owed you $100,000 in expenses incurred and back pay that had been accruing during your employment. Not surprisingly, the owner tried to blame *you* for their misdeeds and mistakes and even sues *you* for mismanagement of a government contract.

Now, you have to hire a lawyer that you can't afford to protect you and your family. You got statements from people in the office, along with a lot of emails between the owner and yourself, that exonerated you of all the false claims. When you give the evidence to your lawyer, he gives you some harsh, but wise advice. "You are not going to like what I have to say. It's painful advice, but I recommend you settle for the $10,000 they are offering you."

Truth be told, continuing this legal battle was not worth the time, energy, legal fees, or a blow to your reputation to let these guys try and take you down. The lawsuit was not yet entered into the court system because the owner did not follow proper legal filing procedures, not to mention their claim was a lie. In the end, your lawyer suggests you take the $10,000 settlement offer.

Now this is where your faith comes in.

You're sitting in your lawyer's office thinking, "it is what it is, God." Of the $10,000 you received, $5,000 went to your lawyer. You went from being owed $100,000 to getting $5,000 and had mud thrown on your character.

A few weeks later, you and your significant other take a walk to the mailbox. You reach into the mailbox and there was a letter from the IRS. "Perfect, a letter from the IRS; this can't be good news," you think to yourself. But instead, it was a surprise refund from years earlier that you overpaid on your taxes. How much did you overpay? $5,000. You laugh and laugh thinking, "Wow, God has a wicked sense of humor."

A few months later, you received a call from a government contracting officer who told you one of their contracts had been terminated and asked if your new company would take it. A few weeks later, the government awards you your first major contract. The contract was long enough that it would help you recoup for the losses from your previous employer.

The moral of this story is there are times when things that appear to be unfair and unjust are actually blessings in disguise. God has you walk through that dark valley so you could not only experience hardship, but more importantly, learn from it. It is a lot easier to help someone who is going through tough times when you have been there yourself.

Wisdom comes from experience. As leaders, we should take all of the struggles and turn them into learning experiences.

In my twenties, before I was a mature Christian, I would ask God "Why me?" when terrible things happen. Sometimes, I would get frustrated and ticked off. The good news is as we get older and mature in our faith, wisdom kicks in. You learn to deal with hurt, pain, disappointment, and betrayals. You can learn through your struggles and come out better, wiser, and stronger on the other side. Over time you learn some absolutes like the truth never changes. You can say all you want. You can make up lies, try, and change the story line, and even produce "alternative facts" but the truth never changes.

As my beloved Pastor Greg would say as he was going through a dark season in his life *"there is value in the struggle."* Rest in peace Pastor Greg.

The biggest thing we can learn during our struggles is to do the right thing and leave the results up to God. As you grow in your faith, doing the right this is always the right answer.

Attitude = 100%

Some leaders you hear, and some leaders you feel.

For the most part, people are emotional human beings, and each person displays their emotions in different ways. There are certain things that trigger emotions—what we see, hear, touch, smell, and personal interactions. Leaders you "hear" can be deemed as "I believe in" the leader at this given time. Leaders you "feel" go a step further with "I trust" the leader, and that is the ultimate goal for any leader—so that your followers actually trust you. When your followers trust you, they will walk with you into the fire! And to build this trust with your followers, it starts with your attitude.

Your attitude is what enables you to turn on your leadership light. Oftentimes we call ourselves leaders, but our leadership light is not on. Now, what your leadership light means is up to you. A lighthouse in a storm with no light serves no purpose.

If sacrifice, humility, selflessness, and the ability to put others before you are not part of who you are, chance are your leadership light is not on. The authentic and servant leader must have an appreciation for the importance and value of effective leadership. Leadership is not a destination, it is a journey that requires continuous practice, learning, and adjustments. Awareness of who you are and what you want to be, and the gap between, can be filled by your attitude.

I have a non-scientific math problem that shows the power of attitude. If you took the letters A through Z and gave each letter a corresponding number, starting with A = one, B = two, C = three, D = four and so on. When you spell the word

KNOWLEDGE with this number system, you score 96. When you spell HARD WORK you score 98. Both of those numbers fall short of 100. But when you spell ATTITUDE, you score a perfect 100.

Remember, as leaders we cannot train attitude. We can teach others how to do the job better. We can inspire others to be a harder worker, but we cannot train another person's attitude. Attitude is internal. For me, my true source is my faith and how and what God created for me in this life. I choose to focus on my blessings, and the positives, and what I can influence.

> *"Finally, brothers, whatever is true, whatever is honorable, whatever is just, whatever is pure, whatever is lovely, whatever is commendable, if there is any excellence, if there is anything worthy of praise, think about these things. What you have learned and received and heard and seen in me— practice these things, and the God of peace will be with you."*
>
> - Philippians 4:8-9 [29]

Too often people let worldly experiences shape their attitude and that's normal. However, once we understand this, and we become aware of the consequences, we can go on a journey to find our true purpose in life. We should remind ourselves that we are not in control of the things life throws our way. God is in control of that, and the struggles He chooses to present us with. You can only control your personal decisions and choices, and the value you will choose to gain from the struggle.

Character, credibility, integrity, honesty, selflessness, and humility are the values that can help foster and maintain positive attitude.

> *"Not one drop of my self-worth depends on your acceptance of me."*
>
> — *Quincy Jones[30]*

Creating A Healthy Attitude

A healthy attitude means you are not closed minded, and you are not carrying others' baggage. An open mind forgives, and an open mind creates new understanding. A healthy attitude is open to discussion. We can agree to disagree. I am not so jaded by the fact that you and I are so different. When you really pull back the curtains, and see all the actors on stage, we have more in common than we think. We agree with each other more than we disagree. That 15 to 20% disagreement is always center stage, and until we learn to open that curtain wider, and take in the other 80% of similarity, we will not make progress.

When it comes to understanding, when people say, "I understand what you're going through," but have not actually gone through it themselves, it's impossible to be sincere because you're not being honest, or authentic.

Instead of saying "I understand what you're going through," you can replace it with "I'll be praying for you." This response is open-minded, unassuming, and indicative of a healthy attitude. It is a statement that does not pass judgment or give unqualified advice.

My wife is my best friend. When my wife is having a difficult day, I've learned over 34 years of marriage, the best way to support her is by not saying much. Instead, I am just there, and I listen. You are never going to go wrong by just being present and listening. From a faith perspective, we live in what I mostly define as a fallen world. Our faith is in control. If you are a true believer, you can always rely on the fact that our faith is in control, and we are not.

In the movie *Bridge of Spies* starring Tom Hanks, Hanks plays a corporate insurance lawyer who is tasked to represent a captured Soviet spy and to negotiate a prisoner exchange during the Cold War. The Soviet spy appears to be unfazed by his pending death sentence. Hanks is surprised and puzzled that is client is so calm and collected and says to him "You don't seem very worried." To which his client responds, "Would it help?"[31] This is how one's faith should work.

Does is it help us to be worried in the face of adversity? Will things change because we worry about things? Absolutely not. Worrying never changes anything (except causing high-blood pressure, loss of sleep etc.). This serenity is another trait of a healthy attitude. We are not built to carry all our and other people's worries because it is simply too much to bear. My faith tells me we must help people. John Wooden, Hall of Fame basketball coach from UCLA says, "There is no way you can have a perfect day unless you help somebody."[32]

This is the final piece in the healthy attitude puzzle. As we rebound from our own struggles, we must pay it forward and help others in the midst of theirs.

We should remind ourselves on a regular basis that there is a purpose in this life journey. There is purpose and value in every struggle. We must travel through the valley to appreciate the peaks. And as we exit life's valleys, we are prepared and ready to help others. There is an adage that if you want to go fast, go alone. If you want to go far, go together.

Here is one of my favorite stories that exemplifies the importance of having a healthy attitude and a balanced perspective about what is important:

There is a tale about this small town in southern Italy, where on the first Saturday of each month they gather in the town square, and they have a race to see who the fastest runner is. For six months in a row, the same young boy won every race. The following month there were no competitors to challenge him. Seeing this unfold, two elderly gentlemen who were in their 80s, decided they would enter the race. Just before the three approached the starting line, the oldest woman in town, who was sitting peacefully under a tree, called the young boy over and said, "it appears to me that you really enjoy winning." The boy replied, "Indeed I do. It's all about winning." The elderly woman added "And it's obvious that you also love to hear the roar of the crowd." "Yes," said the young boy, "what is the point of winning without the cheers?" She motioned for the young boy to come closer; she whispered in his ear **"Today, if you want to hear the roar and cheer of the crowd, finish the race together."**

We become better winners, better competitors, and better humans when we work together during times of struggle.

How have your struggles helped you build your healthy attitude?

CHAPTER 9 TAKEAWAYS

- *"Consider it pure joy, my brothers and sisters, whenever you face trials of many kinds, because you know that the testing of your faith produces perseverance." -James 1:2-4*[33]

- There are times when things that appear to be unfair and unjust are actually blessings in disguise.

- For the most part people are emotional human beings, and each person displays their emotions in different ways.

- If sacrifice, humility, selflessness, and the ability to put others before you are not present, your leadership light is probably not on.

- A healthy attitude means you are not closed minded, and you are not carrying others' baggage.

- We become better winners, better competitors, and better humans when we work together during times of struggle.

Humility; Either You Have it, or You Do not.

"Do nothing from rivalry or conceit, but in humility count others more significant than yourselves. Let each of you look not only to his own interests, but also to the interests of others. Have this mind among yourselves, which is yours in Christ Jesus"

—Philippians 2:3-5 [34]

There are multiple levels of humility, and they vary based on the lens we view them through—how we see ourselves, and how others see us. From a personal lens point of view, we should know ourselves better than anybody else, but sometimes not. Humility is self-awareness to know if we are humble. A good rule of thumb is if you must ask yourself if you're humble, you are probably not.

The other lens, how other people view us, is equally important. If you are thinking "my humility is in check," realize that assessment could be clouded simply because you have no control of how others may see you. In their eyes, you may not be seen as being humble. From a leadership perspective, true humility is centered mostly around one's, character, actions, what we say, and how we say it.

For example, if someone says, "I'm a very humble person." Sure, but can you substantiate that claim? Oftentimes, what some leaders do is only convey their humility through their words, but not with actions or deeds.

Are you humble, or do you just appear to be humble? How do you practice humility?

When I took command of my last Air Force squadron, I got there a little earlier than I should have. My goal at the time was simple: stay out of the way of the current Commander, do not say anything, and just observe. Unfortunately, the current Commander thought he was going to train me how to be a Commander. That is not how it works, and he knew it. During the squadron's weekly staff meeting, my predecessor constantly referred to himself as, "The Commander." Why? Maybe after being in charge for two years, somehow people in his unit forgot he was the squadron commander. Everyone knew that wasn't the case.

During this observation period, my predecessor violated one leadership's cardinal rules, *correct in private and praise in public,* several times. The commander would embarrass members of his staff by calling them out during the meeting for mistakes they had made. I soon realized arriving at the unit early was not a bad thing. It turned out to be a blessing in disguise. It was an opportunity to witness what a lack of humility looks and sounds like up close and personal.

About a month later, I assumed command of the squadron. At our first staff meeting I told the officers and non-commissioned officers (NCOs):

"I'm not the kind of leader you experienced with the former commander. I promise to never embarrass you in public. I will give you the opportunity to speak openly and freely. And if there's something to be said in private, I guarantee you it will be said in private. I trust that all of you are good at your jobs, and you know how to take care of your people, and that is my number one rule for you: Take care of your people."

With those words, I tried to set a new standard and institute a new culture for the entire squadron. Hopefully, my words and actions helped them see me through a different lens, the lens of humility. Do not grade yourself as being humble, that is somebody else's job to do that.

The Humility Equation

Humility + Trust + Healthy Attitude = Character

Just as leaders are building a chocolate cake culture for their business, we can do the same when it comes to humility. The main ingredients for our character cake are humility, trust, and a healthy attitude. You cannot be the effective servant, and transformative leader you want to be without humility.

Similarly, we sometimes have different definitions concerning character and integrity. On occasion, I also use those words interchangeably. Let us unpack it. Character, unlike humility, is one of those things that can vary day to day, and action to action. We have all had high character days, and possibly low character days, because we are imperfect. I think the same can be said for integrity because we tend to rationalize things. The ultimate goal for both character and integrity is consistency. Furthermore, integrity is measured by consistency, particularly by doing the right thing, even when it is an unpopular thing to do. This brings us to reputation, which has a lot to do with one's character. If you are a person of faith, you know that reputation is what other people think of you. Character is what God knows to be true of you. Nothing more, nothing less.

What's Next?

I have come to understand being a leader is a sacred responsibility. You have probably heard the quote "With great power comes great responsibility." If you agree, I strongly encourage you to add the word **accountability** to the quote.

As I mentioned earlier, being a business owner or entrepreneur is hard and not for the faint-hearted. Over the years as a small business owner, leader, and mentor, I have tried to have a better understanding of fear. Is fear a human condition that we all have? Is anyone immune to fear? Tough questions that a lot of people, including me, struggle with. My way of dealing with fear is based on my faith and relationship with God. Here are some of the scripture verses that help me[35]:

> **Isaiah 41:10** - Fear not, for I am with you; be not dismayed, for I am your God; I will strengthen you, I will help you, I will uphold you with my righteous right hand.
>
> **2 Timothy 1:7** - For God gave us a spirit not of fear but of power and love and self-control.
>
> **1 John 4:18** - There is no fear in love, but perfect love casts out fear. For fear has to do with punishment, and whoever fears has not been perfected in love.

Psalm 34:4 - I sought the Lord, and he answered me and delivered me from all my fears.

Joshua 1:9 - Have I not commanded you? Be strong and courageous. Do not be frightened, and do not be dismayed, for the Lord your God is with you wherever you go."

Fear can rob us of time, threaten a leaders' character, integrity, and cause us not to act. That my friends is the goal of leadership—action through influence.

CONCLUSION

I can honestly say the second half of my life journey has been even more exciting the first half. My thoughts and views on retirement have changed dramatically. I stopped calling it retirement and coined a new phrase "reassignment."

Everything I do now outside of Sonoran Technology is fun:

- Spending more time with my family...a whole lot of Smiley family members
- Mentoring and coaching new small business leaders
- Serving on the Arizona Veterans Hall of Fame Society Board
- Working with the Arizona Tuskegee Airmen Youth Program
- Helping Veterans transition to second careers
- Working community leaders on quality-of-life projects
- Serving on the Arizona State University West Valley Campus Leadership Alliance and the Pat Tillman Veterans Center Boards
- Supporting the Arizona Black Philanthropy Initiative (BPI)
- Making the City of Goodyear, Arizona, a great place live, work and play
- Serving on the Honoring America's Veterans (HAV) Advisory Committee

Now, in the second season of my life, I realize how much more I can help create life change by helping small business owners build their version of a chocolate cake, help them take care of people, build their infrastructure, engage their employees, know their employees better, observe the competition, understand the value in the struggle, and better understand the values of trust, integrity, character, communications and humility.

I'm continuing to learn because things continue to change. We are always learning as we mature. As a leadership coach, I am keenly focused on helping the next generation of entrepreneurs and business leaders. The greatest lesson I have that you can learn is from experience, and I look forward to passing those lessons on.

I hope that the *Smiley Leadership and Mentoring Experience* helps you on your life journey. I hope this book serves as a guide as you continue to do important things for your employees, your business, your community, and our nation. The stories in here are written for you. Please share this book with your family, friends, business owners, and entrepreneurs. Finally, whatever you take away from the *Smiley Leadership and Mentoring Experience*, make it your own.

We have our own individual gifts, talents, and blessings.

What are you going to do with yours?

BIBLIOGRAPHY

1 *The holy bible: New international version, containing the old testament and the new testament.* Grand Rapids, MI: Zondervan Bible Publishers, 1978.

2 Gokey, Danny. "Haven't Seen It Yet." YouTube, February 1, 2019. https://www.youtube.com/watch?v=X1eMZiOJ0a0.

3 "The Great Migration." Smithsonian American Art Museum. Accessed April 28, 2024. https://americanexperience.si.edu/wp-content/uploads/2014/07/The-Great-Migration.pdf.

4 "The Great Migration (1910-1970)." National Archives and Records Administration. Accessed April 28, 2024. https://www.archives.gov/research/african-americans/migrations/great-migration#:~:text=The%20Great%20Migration%20was%20one,the%201910s%20until%20the%201970s.

5 Warren, Rick. *The Purpose Driven Life.* Zondervan, 2002.

6 "About PVC." Palm Valley Church. Accessed April 28, 2024. https://palmvalley.org/about-pvc/.

7 Duncan, Rodger Dean. "What If What You Think You Know Just Ain't So?" Forbes, May 31, 2019. https://www.forbes.com/sites/rodgerdeanduncan/2019/05/31/what-if-what-you-think-you-know-just-aint-so/?sh=77f87f24355e.

8 Julian, Larry S. *God is my CEO: Following god's principles in a bottom-line world.* Avon, MA: Adams Media, 2014.

9 Carter, Timothy. "The True Failure Rate of Small Businesses." Entrepreneur, January 3, 2021. https://www.entrepreneur.com/starting-a-business/the-true-failure-rate-of-small-businesses/361350.

10 *A league of their own.* Film. Columbia Pictures, 1992.

11 Moran, Brian. "I Lost My Small Business in the Great Recession, but at Least I Learned How to Prepare for the next One." CNBC, October 21, 2019. https://www.cnbc.com/2019/10/20/i-lost-my-business-in-great-recession-im-prepared-for-next-one.html.

12 Powell, Colin. "Kids Need Structure." Colin Powell: Kids need structure | TED Talk, January 23, 2013. https://www.ted.com/talks/colin_powell_kids_need_structure?language=en.

13 "Employment Situation of Veterans - 2023." Bureau of Labor Statistics. Accessed April 28, 2024. https://www.bls.gov/news.release/pdf/vet.pdf.

14 "The State of Small Business in America." The State of Small Business in America | U.S. Chamber of Commerce, March 8, 2024. https://www.uschamber.com/small-business/state-of-small-business-now.

15 Cox-Ganser, Jean M, and Paul K Henneberger. "Occupations by Proximity and Indoor/Outdoor Work: Relevance to Covid-19 in All Workers and Black/Hispanic Workers." American journal of preventive medicine, May 2021. https://www.ncbi.nlm.nih.gov/pmc/articles/PMC7970652/.

16 Jaiswal, Neeraj Kumar, and Rajib Lochan Dhar. "The Influence of Servant Leadership, Trust in Leader and Thriving on Employee Creativity." Leadership & Organization Development Journal, March 6, 2017. https://www.emerald.com/insight/content/doi/10.1108/LODJ-02-2015-0017/full/html.

17 *Heart of Champions*. Film. Vertical Entertainment, 2021.

18 Kenton, Will. "Hersey-Blanchard Situational Leadership Model: How It Works." Investopedia. Accessed April 28, 2024. https://www.investopedia.com/terms/h/hersey-and-blanchard-model.asp#:~:text=The%20Hersey%2DBlanchard%20Model%20suggests,%2Drelevant%20and%20relationship%2Drelevant.

19 Collins, Jim. *Good to great: Why some companies make the leap ... and others don't*. London: Random House, 2001.

20 Institute, Disney. 1996. "Hiring Right Fit Talent." *Disney Institute Courses*. Orlando, Florida.

21 "Gen Z in the Workplace: How Should Companies Adapt?" John Hopkins University, November 16, 2023. https://imagine.jhu.edu/blog/2023/04/18/gen-z-in-the-workplace-how-should-companies-adapt/#:~:text=Today%2C%20a%20large%20chunk%20of,about%2030%25%20of%20the%20workforce.

22 "Watch: United Aviate Academy's First Graduation January 25, 2023." United Aviate, January 25, 2023. https://www.aviateacademy.com/graduation.

23 Institute, Disney. 1996. "Hiring Right Fit Talent." *Disney Institute Courses*. Orlando, Florida.

24 *The holy bible: New international version, containing The old testament and the new testament*. Grand Rapids, MI: Zondervan Bible Publishers, 1978.

25 *The holy bible: New international version, containing The old testament and the new testament*. Grand Rapids, MI: Zondervan Bible Publishers, 1978.

26 Put, Richard W. "The Origins of SWOT Analysis." Science Direct, February 22, 2023. https://www.sciencedirect.com/science/article/pii/S0024630123000110.

27 *The holy bible: New international version, containing The old testament and the new testament.* Grand Rapids, MI: Zondervan Bible Publishers, 1978.

28 *The holy bible: New international version, containing The old testament and the new testament.* Grand Rapids, MI: Zondervan Bible Publishers, 1978.

29 *The holy bible: New international version, containing The old testament and the new testament.* Grand Rapids, MI: Zondervan Bible Publishers, 1978.

30 "Person of the Week: Quincy Jones." ABC News, December 15, 2006. https://abcnews.go.com/WN/PersonOfWeek/person-week-quincy-jones/story?id=2730571.

31 Spielberg, Steven, Marc Platt, Kristie Macosko Krieger, Matt Charman, Ethan Coen, and Joel Coen. *Bridge of spies.* Film. United States: Walt Disney Studios Motion Pictures, 2015.

32 Resch, Ryan. "John Wooden: The Legendary UCLA Coach's Top 20 Quotes." Bleacher Report, October 3, 2017. https://bleacherreport.com/articles/1072132-john-wooden-the-legendary-ucla-coachs-top-20-quotes.

33 *The holy bible: New international version, containing The old testament and the new testament.* Grand Rapids, MI: Zondervan Bible Publishers, 1978.

34 *The holy bible: New international version, containing The old testament and the new testament.* Grand Rapids, MI: Zondervan Bible Publishers, 1978.

35 *The holy bible: New international version, containing The old testament and the new testament.* Grand Rapids, MI: Zondervan Bible Publishers, 1978.

Printed in the United States
by Baker & Taylor Publisher Services